What Is Theology?

What Is Theology?

—An Orthodox Methodology—

Jean-Claude Larchet

Translated from the French
by Michael Lomax

HOLY TRINITY PUBLICATIONS
Holy Trinity Seminary Press
Holy Trinity Monastery
Jordanville, New York
2023

Printed with the blessing of His Grace,
Bishop Luke of Syracuse
and Abbot of Holy Trinity Monastery

What Is Theology?: An Orthodox Methodology

Authorized translation from the French language edition
by Dr Jean-Claude Larchet, Qu'est-ce que la théologie? Méthodologie
de la théologie orthodoxe dans sa pratique et son enseignement

HTSP
HOLY TRINITY
SEMINARY PRESS

An imprint of

HOLY TRINITY PUBLICATIONS
Holy Trinity Monastery
Jordanville, New York 13361-0036
www.holytrinitypublications.com

ISBN: 978-1-942699-51-4 (paperback)
ISBN: 978-1-942699-56-9 (ePub)

Library of Congress Control Number 2023945504

Cover Photo: "Quill & Inkwell." Source: istockphoto.com,
ID182674539, DNY59; Vector graphic quill: Freepik.com

Psalms are taken from A Psalter for Prayer, trans. David James
(Jordanville, N.Y.: Holy Trinity Publications, 2019).

Contents

Introduction

Studies devoted to the methodology of Orthodox theology are few and far between. The main reason for this is that Orthodox theology came into being spontaneously and not by application of any preestablished methodology.

This is the case of traditional Orthodox theology, as represented by the Fathers, which came into being in response to the various needs of the Church (primarily catechetical, exegetical, and apologetic). It was then transmitted essentially by mimesis, respecting Tradition, that is to say in line with the Fathers and following their spirit.

But this is also the case with modern Orthodox theology which, in one of its important currents, that of *religious philosophy*, has undergone, according to an equally mimetic and most-often unconscious process, the influences of Roman Catholic and Protestant theology,[1] and sometimes also philosophical or spiritualist influences[2] foreign to Christianity.[3] This latter case has given rise to tensions, followed by clarifications of a methodological nature: thus the work of Father Georges Florovsky developed largely as a critique of what he saw as a debasing of and even an estrangement from Orthodox theology, and as an incitement to restore to it its identity.[4] In parallel with him, other Orthodox authors have worked in the same direction, but in a less systematic way, that is to say by preliminary or additional commentaries, and above all by setting an example in their own writings of what they consider to be a correct way—that is to say, in conformity with the Orthodox Tradition—of "doing theology." These clarifications have not prevented the continuing existence of the current inspired by Western theology and philosophy. Certain tendencies of this current have even been accentuated by the closer contacts established between

Orthodox theologians and Catholic and Protestant theologians under the influence of several factors: the development of ecumenical relations during the second half of the twentieth century; the multiplication of university exchanges in the context of international conferences; the opening of borders in the countries of the former communist bloc, and consequently easier access to Western literature and easier access for students from Orthodox countries to Catholic and Protestant theology faculties or to religious training or para-religious institutions of Western academic institutions; the training of a number of teachers from Orthodox educational establishments in Catholic and Protestant faculties in Western Europe; the frequent inviting of teachers of these faculties to Orthodox educational establishments; finally the harmonization of university curricula within the framework of the "Bologna Process."[5] We thus observe today in the training centers (seminaries and theological academies) of the Orthodox countries, an increasingly widespread introduction and influence, in the various fields of theology, of the methodologies from Catholicism and Protestantism. It is clear that certain factors initiated by the Western world may also have played a role in this process: globalization, reflected in the erasing of borders and identities in all areas (except that this phenomenon does not result in a mixing of the elements that are put together, but in a standardization to the exclusive benefit of the Western elements, whose power is dominant); the primary importance given to science, and therefore to scientific or so-called scientific methods, which have imposed themselves, from the physical and biological sciences, onto the domain of the "human sciences" then onto the various branches of theology which have been aligned as closely as possible with the latter and sometimes even reduced to them; and the fascination exerted by the West, for several centuries, among the peoples of the countries of the East and the Balkans, victims of an incomprehensible but real inferiority complex.

The introduction of Catholic and Protestant methodologies,[6] and at times methodologies directly derived from the "human sciences" into the various fields of Orthodox theology have had prejudicial effects on it. They undermine its identity and its specificity, without the introducers and users of these methodologies being cognizant of this, having often been trained in these sciences from the start of their studies before learning—and even often without the possibility of learning—of this identity and this specificity.

This loss or reduction of identity is very serious, because the various fields of Orthodox theology are directly connected to the Orthodox faith and to the Orthodox spiritual experience, and there exists between them a relationship of reciprocal dependence. As several major theologians of our time have suggested (including Father Georges Florovsky and Vladimir Lossky), the form and nature of theology depend on faith and spiritual experience, but the reverse is also true, so that to change the identity of theology is to change faith and spiritual experience.

We can clearly see how, in Catholicism and Protestantism, the systematic and general introduction of scientific methods (or allegedly such) and of the critical approach that is intimately linked to them have considerably modified the relationship between the clergy and the faithful trained through them in the various "subjects" of theology, whether dogma, Scripture, the Liturgy, ethics, the Fathers, or still others that we will examine in this study. The considerable decadence of Protestantism and Catholicism in recent decades[7] is partly explained by these factors, and a similar decadence will not fail to affect Orthodoxy if its clergy are trained in a theology which obeys the same methods, for these methods, borrowed from the secular world, in fact have a secularizing effect and are generators of relativism and agnosticism. Instead of bringing the believer closer to the subject or object of his faith, they distance him from it by creating, as we will see, a critical distance—presented as a virtue by the methods in question and those who adhere to them—the deleterious effects of which are obvious.

The question of methodology is therefore not only or primarily a theoretical question. Because, in the Orthodox Church, theology in its various components is intimately linked to spiritual experience, it is a question of spiritual life and therefore of Life in general. This is why the present work has not only a theoretical but also a practical scope, and is of relevance not only to specialists, but to all the faithful.

While Catholic and Protestant scholars—followed by some Orthodox scholars whom they have trained or influenced—have long exercised their critical spirit against traditional ways of approaching theological subjects in the Orthodox world, to the contrary, this study proposes to subject to critical evaluation the scientific methods which are upheld and practiced by them—or those claimed to be such. It is not a question of completely rejecting these methods which, in certain fields or in part, can be justified and can benefit Orthodox theological subjects both in their teaching and in their practice (especially at the level of research). It is a question of defining in what domains and to what extent, in other words within what limits, these methods are justified and applicable. These limits are defined by taking into account the Orthodox identity of theology and its distinctive components.

Our aim here is not to provide a detailed study, nor to apply our reflection to one or the other educational establishment of a particular local Orthodox Church. Having lectured at various institutions (theology faculties, theological academies, and seminaries) of several Orthodox countries, on the nature of theology (situated historically and in relation to connected subjects), the author has been able to observe that the same problems arise to varying degrees in these different countries and their different educational establishments. We will identify here only a few major principles, relative to the main subjects of theological education, it being also understood that these subjects are variously distributed, divided, subdivided, even named from one establishment to the next.[8]

We are well aware that what is written here is situated in a context of tensions which we have clearly perceived within teaching staff during our meetings with them in the institutions visited, and which we still perceive today in our regular correspondence with teachers from these institutions, whether Russian, Greek, Romanian, Serbian, Lebanese, Bulgarian, or Polish, or even belonging to establishments in the diaspora (in the United States in particular). These tensions already existed in the late nineteenth and early twentieth centuries in Russia, and are described by a historian in the following words: "At the turn of the twentieth century, the debates testify to the meeting of two currents of Russian theology: on the one hand an 'academic' current which defends the scientific vocation of the academies, the role of the positive disciplines and the historical-critical method; and on the other hand, a 'neo-patristic' current borne by scholarly monasticism, concerned with the integration of the spiritual and practical dimension into theology, and a return to biblical sources and to the Fathers of the Church."[9] These two currents have been reinforced in our time by the fact that, as we have seen, various factors have contributed to the development of the so-called scientific tendency.

It seems to us that Orthodox institutions of higher education should stay away from the "sectarianism" which can potentially affect either of these two tendencies[10] and try to make them coexist harmoniously and even collaborate, on the one hand retaining from the scientific methods that which is useful and even necessary to ensure in particular the veracity of the documents to which the various theological subjects refer and to give greater rigor and precision to the studies produced within the framework of these same subjects, while on the other hand taking care to preserve Orthodox identity, respecting the Tradition which ensures its permanence.[11]

Chapter I

Theology: Original Nature, Subsequent Evolutions, and Shapes

1. Theology in Its Most Elevated Sense: Mystical Theology

When we read the texts of the most classical Fathers (the Cappadocians, St Maximus the Confessor, etc.), we see that they give a mystical sense to the word *theology* (θεολογία). From the fourth century onwards especially (but this distinction already existed in Origen), the Fathers generally consider that the spiritual life is made up of two degrees: *praxis,* which designates the ascetic life in the broad sense, and *gnosis* (γνῶσις) or knowledge. *Gnosis* in turn is subdivided into two degrees: the *physikè theoria* (φυσικὴ θεωρία), or natural contemplation, which is the knowledge of God from His manifestations in creation, and *theology. Theology* is direct knowledge of God. Not of course a knowledge of God according to His essence (because this remains absolutely unknowable) but a knowledge of God according to His energies.[12] *Theoria* (θεωρία) is a knowledge which can be accomplished by the intellect (νοῦς) of man and to a certain extent by his reason (although such knowledge is conditional on purity of intellect and heart as well as freedom from passions). *Theology,* on the contrary, cannot be the work of either reason or intellect, for it is a knowledge of divine realities which are beyond nature and which no natural faculty has the capacity to grasp by its own activity. It can only be the fruit of divine activity (ἐνέργεια), literally "in-working." This knowledge comes about first in the intellect and then in the other human faculties, but they only play the role of receptacle. It is the divine energy itself, communicated to man from the Father, by the Son in the Holy Spirit, which brings about this knowledge. For the divine energy to work in him, man must not only be pure, but have renounced the exercise of the natural energy of his own faculties. That is why those who have had this knowledge say that it was given to them by the Holy Spirit, that they feel in themselves the presence and the action of the Holy Spirit, or that they have in them the "mind of Christ" (cf. 1 Cor 2:16), or that it is no longer they who live but it is Christ who lives in them (cf. Gal 2:20). *Theology*, which is a supernatural revelation of divine mysteries, is a mystagogy (μυσταγωγία). For this reason it is often known as "mystical theology" or "mystagogical theology." In its highest degree, it corresponds to the vision of God, which is accomplished in and by the uncreated divine Light and which is deifying. It is because of the close relationship that exists between the vision of God and the prayer of the heart practiced in its perfection—a relationship underlined by hesychast theology—that Evagrius Ponticus was able to say: "If you are a theologian, you really pray, and if you really pray, you are a theologian."[13]

We understand that this experience of *theologia* is rare, which only saints have. It is experienced only by a few people in a generation, who do not always talk about their experience, which is moreover ineffable. Indeed, words are always limited and apply to finite realities, whereas mystical theology corresponds to an experience of realities which go beyond nature and which are infinite; it is also a knowledge that goes beyond reason and therefore cannot be designated by concepts, nor therefore expressed by words.

If we were therefore to limit theology to *theologia*, as some Orthodox monks sometimes do from a maximalist perspective, theology would become de facto almost nonexistent. However, the omnipresence of theology in the life and history of the Church shows us that theology does not consist only in *theologia*.

It remains true, however, that *theologia* can and should to some extent serve as a model or paradigm for theology. *Theologia* must be the aim and the culmination of theology, with the latter taking on its ultimate meaning and its value only through the former.

2. The Practice of Theology in the Church: Catechetical, Apologetic, and Doxological Theology

Outside of this very lofty meaning, accessible in fact to a very small number of the faithful, theology, right from the first centuries, took three other forms, which are also expressed by the Greek word *theologia* taken in the broad sense of "word" or "speech" (λόγος) concerning God (θεός), the theologian (θεολόγος) being "he who speaks of God."

a. At the Origins of Theology: Catechetical Theology

Theology can be said to have first taken the form of catechesis. Catechesis is, of course, a vast whole covering different areas of Christian faith and spiritual life, but it is obvious that discourse about God holds an essential place in it, and that indeed everything comes back to this.

Catechesis was originally the function of the bishop, of whom teaching is a primary responsibility. It was carried out within the church itself, for the faithful during the liturgy, and outside of it for catechumens.

When parishes were created, the priests, as delegates of the bishops, ensured this catechetical function, which later on was also exercised by lay people delegated by bishops or priests. Origen (second century), to cite but one well-known example, was one such layman. It should, however, be noted in passing that the canons of the Church did not give the laity the possibility of preaching in church, nor even, it seems, of teaching publicly outside it, and that some canons deny this possibility also to clerics (priests and deacons), reserving it only for bishops.[14]

Many patristic works (e.g., those of St Cyril of Jerusalem or St John Chrysostom) take the form of homilies, the intent of which is clearly catechetical. Certain works by great theologians, such as the *Exact Exposition of the Orthodox Faith* of St John Damascene, also belong to the genre of catechetical theology, intended for the instruction not only of children or adults who become Christians, but also of all the faithful who wish to deepen their faith, and which can be also used to make known the Orthodox faith to those who are outside the Church.

b. The Historical Necessity of Apologetic Theology

A second form taken by theology is the apologetic form, that is, consisting in the defense of the faith. This form of theology has two aspects: that of refuting heresies, and a correlative aspect of explaining the true faith. It can be said that most of the theological writings left to us by the Fathers fall within this form of theology.

This form of theology is not freely chosen by the theologian. It is always imposed by circumstances. Very early in the Church there appeared heresies, that is, wrong ways of conceiving God and speaking of Him. These heresies were not only an "insult to God," but they endangered the life of the Church and compromised the salvation of the faithful. It was therefore essential to refute them.

This necessity imposed the use of methods capable of effecting this refutation. Once the task became that of convicting heretics of their errors or of convincing any of the faithful tempted to follow them, it was often essential for theology to resort to a rational way of thinking, using the rules of logic and demonstrating the qualities that any rational discourse requires: rigor, coherence, precision, clarity. Examining the writings of the Fathers that are directed against heresies, we see that they use rational procedures based on demonstration. One of their favorite processes is to demonstrate, by resorting to the basic rules of logic (the principle of non-contradiction, the principle of the excluded middle ...), the contradictory character of certain affirmations of the heretics, or the absurd consequences which result. Since heresies are "twisted" and "confusing" ways of understanding the truths of faith, theology, in refuting them, is forced to take detours it would not otherwise take. It is also obliged to use vocabulary adapted to that of the heretics that it would not otherwise use, or to resort to the vocabulary of philosophy to make new distinctions or to more precisely explain the content of true faith. All in all, it often ends up at a level of abstraction and complexity that it would otherwise avoid. If, for example, the thought of St Maximus the Confessor seems so complicated, it is because, in attempting to justify their false conceptions of a single energy or a single will of Christ, the Monoenergists and Monothelites developed theories that were at once very subtle and very confused. We see that when St Maximus is not obliged to adapt to the discourse of heretics, he has a very clear form of thought and expression, as in his *Centuries on Charity* or his *On the Ascetic Life*. Another example is the difference between the complex works of St Gregory Palamas wherein he refutes the false conceptions of Barlaam and Akindynos, and the homilies he gave at the end of his life as archbishop of Thessalonica, which are remarkably clear and simple, while expressing exactly the same theology.

c. Doxological Theology

A third form of theology is doxological theology, that is, a theology of praise.

This form of theology is found in certain patristic works. The best-known are the *Poems* of St Gregory of Nazianzus (known in the Orthodox tradition as Gregory the Theologian) and the *Hymns* of St Symeon the New Theologian. We can note in passing that these Fathers are the only ones, along with St John the Evangelist, to have received in the Church the qualifier, affixed to their name, of "theologian." Why? St John was not a greater theologian than Sts. Luke, Matthew, Mark or Paul. St Gregory the Theologian was not a greater theologian than St Basil the Great, nor was St Symeon the New Theologian a greater theologian than St Gregory Palamas. We cannot consider that they were called "theologians" because they had the experience of *theologia*—the vision of God. Other Fathers had the vision of God and were not called "theologians." This qualifier, while presupposing and expressing the direct and very high knowledge and experience of God that they had, is due above all to the form of some of their writings: a poetic form, which uses many metaphors and symbols. This language is undoubtedly the one that best suits theology. Not only does its beauty bear witness to the Beauty of God, but the symbols it uses at once reveal God and preserve His mystery; they thus manifest together the two dimensions, cataphatic and apophatic, which theology must have.

Cataphatic theology (also called positive theology) is that which proceeds by affirmations about God, revealing the qualities of God that He manifests in His uncreated energies. Apophatic theology (also called negative theology) is that which proceeds by negations, emphasizing that God has nothing in common with any created being, that His qualities are beyond what we can think or imagine (that He is not beautiful like things that are beautiful, because He is infinitely more beautiful than all beautiful things, He is not good like men are good, because He is infinitely more good than the best men, etc.), and to indicate what He is in His essence absolutely unknowable and inexpressible. It will also be noted that these writings often take the form of prayers. In them, theological knowledge, spiritual experience, and prayer are closely united.

Doxological theology is also that contained in the liturgical texts. We find there a beauty of style and the abundant use of symbols and metaphors. These texts, in most cases poetic compositions, are intended primarily for contemplation and prayer. At the same time they have a dogmatic content. They are therefore an expression of the Orthodox faith which also has an important apologetic and catechetical function, and therefore possesses a certain fullness.

In liturgical services too, theology is closely associated with spiritual experience and prayer. But it is also closely linked to ecclesial life, which reminds us that theology cannot be dissociated from the life, experience, and faith of the whole Church.

3. The Birth and Development of Speculative Theology

a. Genesis

We have just seen that theology, in the first centuries, was never gratuitous, in other words was not undertaken for its own sake, but always responded to a triple necessity: to educate Christians; to defend and to this end to clarify the faith; to praise God.

In the Middle Ages a new form of theology appeared and developed in the Latin West, which did not correspond to any of the previous aims, did not respond to any external need, but only to the individual projects of theologians wishing to develop new systems on the basis of original ideas. Theology becomes speculation, involving to a great extent the reason but also to the creativity—the inventiveness and the imagination—of the theologian. With these characteristics, theology moved away from its primitive nature, becoming closely related on the one hand to philosophy—taking an abstract and systematic form, and proposing a new system of interpretation, starting out from the preceding systems, but concerned to move beyond them—and on the other hand to literature—with the individual inventiveness and originality specific to artistic creation.

Thomas Aquinas is in the medieval Latin world a well-known example of this new way of theologizing: he attaches high value to reason, develops a speculative system of a philosophical type based on the philosophy of Aristotle and strongly centered on the notion of Being (his theology/philosophy taking the form of what Heidegger critically called an "ontotheology"). His system gave rise to developments of a similar type in what we now call a "scholastic" framework. But the West subsequently came to know other similar systems. In line with its liberal conception of emphasizing the individual reading and interpretation of Scripture, Protestantism took this "free" and creative way of doing theology much further. This way of conceiving and of practicing theology has marked the whole Latin world up to the present day, the greatest theologians of the twentieth century are considered such because of their supposed creativity.

It is only in the nineteenth century that speculative theology appeared in the Orthodox world, along with the characteristics that we have just presented. There was certainly previous to this—from the seventeenth century in Russia—an influence of Latin, and in particular scholastic theology, but this influence was exercised above all on the form of the teaching or the exposition of theology and concerned, in substance, only a few specific and secondary points. It was mainly under the influence of German philosophy that theology in Russia took the form of what is commonly called "religious philosophy," in which abstract rational speculation, the creation of new systems of interpretation, and the high esteem given to the creative freedom of the theologian became dominant. Sophiology, developed by V. Soloviev, P. Florensky, and S. Bulgakov, inspired by Western influences, at once philosophical (German idealism), pseudo-mystical/esoteric (the sophiology of Jakob Böhme), and theological (Protestantism and Roman Catholicism) is its most emblematic representative.[15]

The philosophical, speculative, and creative character of Orthodox theology as can be observed in the Greek theology of the twentieth century is also the result of influences foreign to the Orthodox Tradition. This is particularly the case of the dogmatic theology elaborated by C. Androustos, P.N. Trembelas, and their disciples, which reflects a strong influence of Latin scholasticism. This is also the case of the theology of the 1960s among the authors gravitating around the journal *Synaxi*, and particularly in the personalist current represented by C. Yannaras and J. Zizioulas, marked by a strong influence of the existentialist/personalist current of Russian religious philosophy (N. Berdiaev), but also of the existentialist/personalist current of Russian philosophy (M. Buber, E. Lévinas) and atheistic existentialism (M. Heidegger, J.P. Sartre).[16]

Today certain Orthodox theologians remain strongly tempted to engage, under the pretext of openness or dialogue or even out of a desire for novelty, in certain paths of modern Western theology, to adopt more or less consciously their methods and style (almost always speculative), and to be influenced by their content. In the United States, Greece, and Russia, a number of young theologians seem to be attracted to the Protestant theologies and especially the Roman Catholic "new theology" which developed in the second half of the twentieth century. We see that the few Orthodox authors who have tackled the issues raised by these modern theologies have caused Orthodox theology to drift into a speculative style which is fundamentally foreign to it.[17] The desire of certain theologians to enter into dialogue with modern secular (Marxism, Lacanian psychoanalysis, structuralism, etc.) or postmodern thought (deconstructivism) has—quite apart from the fact that this dialogue has proved illusory and vain, not arousing interest in Orthodox religious thought from almost any potential interlocutor—led to an even greater drift in the form and content of theology in the direction of an intellectualist religious philosophy to the point of being abstruse and is far removed from any spiritual experience.

b. Theology and Philosophy

Faced with the confusion of genres affecting the theological currents we have just mentioned, it is necessary to recall the difference that exists between theology and philosophy, and the distance that the former must keep in relation to the latter.

We have seen that, in order to respond effectively to heresies, apologetic theology often had to use a rational-type discourse, respecting not only the rules of logic, but also the qualities of rational thought, and had to resort to concepts borrowed from philosophy.

To do this, it is useful that theologians who practice this form of apologetic theology have philosophical training. Such training is also essential for better understanding the concepts and thought processes of the heretics, but also the apologetic writings of the Fathers whose thought is complex and makes abundant use of abstract concepts of a philosophical type. For example, a philosophical education can considerably improve one's access to the works of Dionysius the Areopagite, St Maximus the Confessor, or St Gregory Palamas. It is therefore legitimate that, in theological training, the historical and practical study of philosophy has always been considered as a useful and even indispensable prerequisite.[18]

But despite this we should not confuse theology and philosophy. They have very different foundations, methods, and goals.

Philosophy is a discipline which is based entirely on reason, and which therefore has its source solely in man's faculty of natural reflection. Theology uses reason as an instrument, but is based on data which does not come from reason itself but from Revelation, as it is known by Tradition, that is to say together from the Holy Scriptures, the apostolic preaching (the so-called kerygma), the writings of the Holy Fathers, the Definitions of Faith of the Councils, and generally the teaching of the Church.

Philosophical reflection constructs its object based entirely on the creative and deductive capacities of reason. Theology, on the contrary, describes an already-given "object." Its efforts are not intended to bring about a new theory or a "new truth," but to explain, for those who do not understand them or misunderstand them, the truths of the faith transmitted by the Church as communicated to it by Christ and the Holy Spirit.

While in history new philosophies constantly appear which challenge previous philosophies—each philosophy, said Leibniz, being built on the ruins of the previous one—there are not, in the very bosom of the (Orthodox) Church, new theologies that add to each other and oppose each other, but new expressions of the same theology.

While the greatness of a philosopher is due to his having invented a new theory, a new vision of the world, the greatness of a theologian comes from his having been able to defend the same Truth against conceptions which distorted it (in other words heresies) or to express the same Truth in a language adapted to that of the men of his time, or to highlight aspects of this same Truth responding to the particular needs of his day.

Finally, philosophy starts from questions to lead, through all sorts of reflexive detours, to new questions. The philosopher Bertrand Russell, for example, writes: "The value of philosophy is to be sought largely in its very uncertainty." Theology, for its part, starts from certainties, those of faith, to end up again with these certainties, seeking only to better establish them in relation to what questions them; to clarify them in relation to what renders them unclear, and to explain them in relation to false interpretations that have taken advantage of the implicit and ambiguous nature of previous formulations.

c. Theology and Literature

Because the emphasis on individual creativity by the representatives of "religious philosophy" is based on a confusion with what characterizes not only philosophy but also literature, and also because the theological works of the Fathers are sometimes, in the Protestant or Catholic universities, assimilated to literary works and studied as such,[19] it is also useful to show what differentiates theology from literature.

There is a literary dimension in theological writings, which justifies the fact that the learning of rhetoric has always constituted, like the learning of philosophy, a prerequisite for the study and practice of theology.[20]

With regard to doxological theology, we have seen that this uses a poetic style, resorting to symbols and metaphors. We are therefore led to ask ourselves what distinguishes it from literature.

We can say first that literary talent is very useful to this form of theology. Like the beauty of music or that of iconographic representations, the beauty of style helps manifest the Beauty of God. It also has the power to touch the heart, and therefore to lead more easily to adherence to the truths expressed by the poetic compositions, and to make it easier to pray not only with the spirit but again with the heart.

We know that talent cannot be learned. It is a gift. In the case of literature, it is a gift that is described as "natural," but which is often the result of particular psychological dispositions formed during childhood and which are sometimes troubled (being linked to conflict, trauma, or disturbing family factors). In the case of theology, it is a charism, a gift of the Holy Spirit.

Moreover, talent, in the case of a secular writer, is a purely individual ability, whereas in the case of a hymnographer, it is an ability that is related to the function that God has called him to exercise in the Church.

Literature is the fruit of the author's imagination. It expresses his or her feelings, desires, phobias, anxieties, inner conflicts, aggressiveness, passions, and so on, but it also expresses the unconscious with its dark sides.

Literature expresses above all, by its content and its form, the individual who is its author; it puts him or her forward as having value. Like any form of art, it is above all an exaltation of the artist himself. When appreciated, it establishes and maintains the fame and glory of the artist.

Doxological theology is in no way at the service of its author, who completely disappears behind the truths he expresses. These truths are not individual "truths," nor expressions of personal psychological states, nor products of the imagination, nor an expression of the unconscious, but the universal Truth which the Church also expresses by other means available to it, such as iconography, preaching, or other forms of theology.

The "mystical theologians" we have mentioned, like St Gregory the Theologian or St Symeon the New Theologian, certainly in their poems and their hymns share a personal experience, and they do so with a personal style. But we see that, in the expression of this personal experience, their individuality is completely effaced, that they make themselves entirely transparent to the supernatural revelations which they have received from the Holy Spirit, and that they testify not of themselves but of God to whom they are united and who is united to them. Most of the hymns in which St Symeon the New Theologian shares his mystical experiences quickly turn into prayers of praise. The personal prayer of these saints then takes the same form as the prayer of the Church, and moreover in many cases the hymns of praise of the saints have been integrated into the liturgical services where they are no longer distinguishable from the other compositions.

These considerations on philosophy and literature lead us to specify the respective places of fidelity to Tradition and creativity in theology, a subject discussed since the first decades of the twentieth century and which is still ongoing.

4. The Conditions for Practicing Theology in an Orthodox Setting

a. The Need for Theology to Be Faithful to Tradition

According to the traditional Orthodox conception, the very first quality of the theologian is fidelity to Tradition.

The three pillars of Tradition are Sacred Scripture, the Councils, and the Fathers. They are intimately linked and mutually enlighten each other. It can be said that everything we know about God is found in the Holy Scriptures, but we know that the Holy Scriptures remain, on certain subjects, implicit or ambiguous. We know that pseudo-Christian sects rely heavily on the Scriptures, and that all heretics claim that their ideas are based on the Holy Scriptures. The Holy Scriptures therefore need to be interpreted and their formulations explained. It is for this purpose that the writings of the Fathers and the Definitions of the Councils exist. But we know that the Councils did not pronounce on all the truths of the faith, but only on those which were contradicted or deformed by heresies. Nor are the Councils a sufficient foundation for the knowledge of God and theology. They must be completed by what Holy Scripture tells us and by the teaching of the Holy Fathers.

The writings of the Holy Fathers, although they speak about almost everything concerning the Christian faith and although they are often very precise and very explicit, nevertheless need to be read and interpreted in the light of Scripture and the Councils, because we know that heretics cite the Fathers extensively, which means that there can also be a heterodox reading of the Fathers.

However, it is possible to have a deep knowledge of each—of Scripture, the Councils, and the Fathers—and to draw from them a teaching that is not Orthodox. It is therefore necessary to emphasize that another fundamental condition of fidelity to Tradition is fidelity to the teaching of the Church, which is conceived in the Orthodox Church as that of the Church in her catholicity. The word catholicity is taken here in its etymological sense: *kath'olon* which means "according to the whole." Catholic is opposed not only to what is partial, but to what is particular, individual. It refers not only to a spatial totality or universality, but also a temporal totality, which includes the past, the present, and the future. We must recall here the fundamental principle stated by St Vincent of Lérins: "In the Catholic Church itself, care must be taken to hold fast to what has been believed everywhere, always, and by all."[21] This is why Tradition is not, as is sometimes thought, fixed on the past alone and is not the mere repetition of the past, although it is always faithful to it. It expresses the faith of the Church beyond time, the permanent faith of the Church, which is fundamentally the faith in Christ who "is the same yesterday, today and forever" (Hebrews 13: 8). We can thus say that the theology in conformity with Tradition is a theology that is in continuity and in harmony with the theology of the past, but also with the theology of the future which will express the same immutable Truth in a form which fully respects it.

The Church's teaching is learned not only in books. It is a living teaching because the Church has the living consciousness of its own immutable and eternal faith (and, one might add, using a famous formula of Vladimir Lossky, it is secondarily the critical spirit of the

Church vis-à-vis what is not this faith). It is therefore only through life in the Church and through personal experience of what she teaches in her catholicity that the theologian can acquire and assimilate the Church's teaching. It is animated by this consciousness, acquired as a faithful member of the Church living in communion with all the other members, with the head of the whole body which is Christ and with the Holy Spirit who animates the whole body, that the theologian will be able to testify to the faith of the Church, to defend it, to expound it, to explain it, and to accomplish any theological activity. If the theologian thinks in an individualistic, particularizing way, positing himself as the source of his thought and seeking to be original—instead of conforming to the Catholic consciousness that the Church has of itself in its totality and of thinking as a member of the body of Christ united with all the other members and in solidarity with them, and united also with the Head—he will inevitably stray into the paths of heresy, which is traditionally understood to be, prior to being an error, a separation from the Body of the Church. Heresy is always the expression of dissidence and an individualistic approach, of a break and separation from the Church as a whole.

b. Value and Limits of Creativity in Theology

Because Tradition is itself the living awareness that the Church, in her catholicity, has of her own faith, which she possesses and transmits from generation to generation, fidelity to Tradition does not amount to conservatism, which is an (often fear-induced) retreat into past expressions of Truth. Absolute respect for the content of the faith must coexist in the theologian with the capacity to express this content in new ways if circumstances so require. This is what the very life of the Church teaches us from its origins. The words "essence," "nature," "hypostasis," and even the word "Trinity" are absent from the Holy Scriptures. The appearance of heresies forced theologians to create new words and, over many centuries, to further develop and give new expression to its Trinitarian theology and Christology in order to explain and specify the Christian faith. Each era and each society has its own specific problems which require the Church to respond to them in appropriate terms. Theology needs therefore to demonstrate a certain creativity, both because the Church is a living organism and because the world in which it lives is constantly evolving. But that does not mean that theology should adopt the ideas of the world, or even the language of the world. Nor does it mean that theology must of necessity develop the world's content, progress, and therefore innovate.

Theological creativity, therefore, is opposed to conservatism, but does not identify itself with a modernist attitude, which consists of a fascination with the contemporary world, borne along by its ideas and behaviors, and systematically promoting the creation of new conceptions. Theological creativity is also opposed to progressivism, which has become a dominant ideology in the modern world (particularly under the influence of science, technology, and the economy, whose indefinite increase is its driving force and its goal), which makes progress into an absolute value and considers all progress to be good *per se*, simply because it is progress.

Creativity in theology should never concern the content of faith itself; it must bear only on the way in which it is expressed. Novelty in theology can never be innovation. It serves to make more explicit a dogma, not in a progress of dogma. Traditional Orthodox theology does not accept the Roman Catholic conception of a development of dogma formulated in the nineteenth century by Cardinal J.H. Newman; it has always been opposed to innovations bearing on the content of the faith, and has fought them when a certain number of these innovations have appeared in Latin theology from the ninth century onwards.

In this process of rendering more explicit, theology is obliged to resort to new concepts which it often borrows from past or contemporary philosophies. But it always "digests" these new expressions and gives them a Christian meaning, thus putting them at the service of the expression of the Truth. In the same way, theology incorporates words of the current language and also uses them in translations of liturgical texts.

The theologian must however take care that these new concepts do not become so dominant as to constitute a system or an ideology which replaces traditional theology or modifies its balance, because then the risk is great of generating errors, heresies, or even pan-heresies.[22] This we see, for example, in the sophiology of Sergei Bulgakov where Sophia is elevated to such an extent that it ends up appearing as a kind of fourth hypostasis of the Trinity.[23] We also see it in the personalism, developed from the modern personalist and existentialist philosophies of Christos Yannaras and John Zizioulas, who, by elevating to the extreme the notion of "person" understood in a particular sense, put it in opposition to essence and nature and devalue the latter, and in so doing break the subtle balance worked out over several centuries by Orthodox triadology and Christology, resulting in multiple errors.[24]

c. The Spiritual Preconditions for the Practice of Theology

The preceding considerations lead us to define the spiritual qualities required of a theologian, according to the traditional Orthodox conception.

Theology is a service of the Church, that is, it is an activity aimed at serving God, all members of the Church, and beyond them all men and women in the world to whom the Truth revealed by Christ and represented by Him is addressed.

This means that the two main qualities of the theologian must be the love of God and neighbor, and humility.

The theologian must show humility because he must completely efface himself before the Truth that he expresses, before the Church which, in its totality, is the holder of this Truth, and before God who is Himself this Truth.

The practice of theology must never proceed from an individual initiative nor express an individual understanding of truth. It is always driven by circumstances, by the needs of the Church at a particular time, and it is under divine inspiration that the theologian should set about doing theology. Unlike art, theology is not an activity one is free to undertake at one's own bidding, following one's personal desire or inspiration.

Humility is the other precondition of the practice of theology, excluding any desire by the theologian to promote himself, to make a name for himself or to draw glory from his work by developing, for example, a new idea or a new doctrine. Heresies have their source in misunderstandings of one or other aspect of the faith, but also in the pride of the pseudo-theologians from whom they originate. This pride manifests itself not only in the desire to innovate, but also in the attitude which consists in setting oneself up as a judge of Tradition, in relativizing the decisions of the Councils, and in judging the thought of the Fathers as if they were profane authors, placing oneself on an equal footing with them, and even—which is not uncommon—considering oneself superior to them in knowledge or intelligence.

Humility, on the contrary, translates into a profound respect for the words of Holy Scripture, the decisions of the Councils, and the writings of the Fathers. The theologian must always desire to situate himself in the continuity of their teaching and always ask himself if what he says and writes is in conformity with the Tradition of the Church as a whole (in its catholicity). All the Fathers give us the example of such an attitude.[25]

Finally, humility is essential for the theologian to avoid the pretension (and the illusion) of knowing everything about God. Humility inspires in him a respect for mystery, a permanent awareness that God is unknowable in His essence and that the richest, most beautiful, and deepest expressions will always only poorly reveal what He is.

It is by consistently living in this spirit of humility, steeped in the Holy Scriptures and the writings of the Holy Fathers, and by living at the heart of the Church that the theologian is trained in theology and acquires what must guide all his activity: an Orthodox consciousness and a real "instinct for Orthodoxy" which allow him to keep himself in the truth, and at the same time to notice what is foreign to the Orthodox faith, impairs it, and endangers it.

This "theological discernment" is acquired not merely by an intellectual reading of the Holy Scriptures and the writings of the Holy Fathers, but by a spiritual reading, undertaken with the intellect and the reason united with the heart, in a spirit of both humility and prayer.

Prayer is, in a general way, indispensable for receiving from God the grace necessary for the practice of true theology. We have already quoted the well-known formula of Evagrius Ponticus establishing an inseparable link between theology and prayer: "If you are a theologian, you truly pray, and if you truly pray, you are a theologian."[26]

Indeed, the practice of true theology is a charism, a gift granted to certain of the faithful by the Holy Spirit for the service of the Church (cf. 1 Cor 12:28–30). Charisms are given by God to particular members of the faithful at particular times in response to a particular need of the Church. Sometimes these faithful are worthy of the charisms they receive, sometimes they receive them before they are worthy, but then they must immediately strive to make themselves as worthy as possible.

Theology assumes that he who exercises it leads a life in conformity with the One to whom he testifies. This means that he must practice the commandments of Christ, in other words strive, in what is called the ascetic life, to fight against the passions and to live according to the virtues, because to live according to the virtues is to live according to Christ who is, as St Maximus the Confessor said, "the essence of all the virtues" of which the Holy Spirit is the giver.

Only the fight against the passions enables the theologian to acquire the interior purity essential to a correct theological approach, and to become worthy of receiving the grace which inspires such an approach. Humility and charity, which we have presented as essential virtues for the theologian, are traditionally placed by the Fathers at the top of the hierarchy of virtues and therefore assume the practice of all the others, as well as the fight against all the passions that oppose them and prevent their emergence.

Orthodoxy is inseparable from orthopraxy (just as, conversely, orthopraxy is inseparable from orthodoxy). Only by leading an upright and just life can the theologian have upright and just thought and speech.

We therefore see that theology, from the viewpoint of those who practice it, is inseparable from spiritual life as a whole, with this spiritual life itself inseparable from life in the Orthodox Church from which the Christian draws the grace without which his solitary effort would be nothing.

5. The Birth and Development of Academic Theology

It was only later that theology became a teaching subject, in connection with the training of clerics (and, later, of teachers and researchers) in an institutional setting—schools and universities.

This process began in the Western Latin world in the twelfth century, with the setting up of faculties of theology. It appeared only much later in the Eastern Orthodox world: in the seventeenth century in the case of Russia, the nineteenth century in Greece and Romania, in the twentieth century in Serbia and Bulgaria.

"Until [these] period[s], in the East, theology and its teaching had never been given the status of an 'institutional academic science.'"[27] The theological training of the clergy was provided in bishops' houses or in monasteries,[28] taking the form primarily of a more perfected catechesis dispensed by Elders, as well as contributions of ecclesial life (in particular liturgical[29]), of monastic life and of personal spiritual life, in which the thorough reading of Scripture and the assiduous reading of the Fathers (whose works constituted a reference and a model) played a fundamental role.[30]

In the nineteenth and twentieth centuries, theological training establishments have, in most cases, been integrated into universities, and therefore organized according to their structures of the latter. In Russia, theological academies remained outside the universities but were structured more or less on university models.

The fact of being taught in an institutional school or university framework has had important consequences for the nature and form of theology.

First of all, it has acquired a more abstract, more conceptual, more rational, and more systematic form, on the one hand in line with the Catholic and Protestant scholastics (who alternately influenced Russian theology from the sixteenth century onwards). On the other hand in line with school and university subjects. For this reason too, it has often come close to philosophy and even at times become mixed and confused with it (in particular in the so-called Russian religious philosophy which flourished in the nineteenth and twentieth centuries in Russia itself, then in the emigration, but also in Greece, up to the present day, among a certain number of theologian-teachers). The constitution of faculties of theology in the same way as other faculties in state universities has often had the consequence of conforming them as much as possible to the scientific models and criteria which these other faculties obeyed. For all these reasons, theology has lost its original essential link with the liturgical and spiritual life, to the point that there has been a real divorce between the former and the latter, as Father Georges Florovsky has noted. Theology has also lost two traditional forms that we have previously described: its apologetic form and its doxological form, which do not fit well with the descriptive form of academic theology and the desire for noncommitment that accompanies the pretension to conform it to scientific standards or, more simply, to harmonize it with other university subjects of a lay and secular character.

Another very important consequence is that theology has been broken down into a multitude of subjects, at times further subdivided into sub-subjects. The number and designation of these subjects vary from one faculty or academy to another, but there are points in common between them. There are also points in common with Catholic or Protestant higher education establishments (institutes or faculties), which in a number of cases have served as models. The presence or absence of certain subjects, as well as the diversity of their naming testifies, however, to specificities, whilst their order of presentation in the curricula is also indicative of certain options or orientations, as we will see in the course of our analyses of these subjects.

Let us note for the moment that this fragmentation of theology into different subjects and these divisions and subdivisions are artificial and modify the nature and form of theology as well as the way of conceiving and practicing it.

Remaining in the sphere of Orthodox theology, we can see that the study of the Bible, dogmatic theology, liturgical theology, ascetic theology, the history of the Church, and ethics were not separate or even distinguished in the ancient conception and practice of the Fathers and the first systems of clerical training. They were rightly considered to imply and include each other in an inseparable whole. Read, for example, a homily of St John Chrysostom. We see clearly that exegesis, hermeneutics, ascetics, dogmatics, ethics, liturgy, hagiology, and Church history are linked. A book like St Maximus the Confessor's *Questions to Thalassios* is at once exegetical and hermeneutic, ascetic, ethical, and dogmatic.

The separation of the different subjects and their extreme specialization has had an effect analogous to that of the specialization of medicine into different branches: we end up no longer seeing how one organ links with the others and we no longer see the organism as a whole.

The separation of the different subjects has also favored their development according to independent and sometimes discordant methods. It has also opened the door to the influence on some of these methods of a methodology foreign to Orthodoxy and sometimes even to Christianity. It has led to their secularization, considerably altering their original meaning and function, and sometimes even their essence. This is the case, for example, of patrology, which has been placed into molds taken from literature or history. The same applies to exegesis, which has been placed into molds provided by literature, philology, linguistics, history, and even psychoanalysis.

The existence of different sectors or different streams is certainly concordant with the demands of "more advanced" teaching, and the scientific methods developed in the Western university world since the seventeenth century are certainly useful and fully justified in certain areas. But it is essential to maintain—or to reconstitute—the links that exist between the different subjects in the Orthodox Tradition, and which in the eyes of the latter belong to the essence of theology. It is also important to set limits on the use of methods that debase the nature of certain subjects as conceived by the Orthodox Tradition.

In any case, it is important to preserve the Orthodox identity of all the subjects that constitute theology as a whole. Otherwise, there is a risk of assimilating them to the way these subjects are conceived—often very differently—in the Catholic and Protestant worlds. They will then be led rapidly along the path of secularization followed by the latter, becoming in the process scarcely distinguishable from profane university subjects, now emptied of their sacred substance, that is of their essential links with faith and Revelation and, more fundamentally, with a transcendent reality, which the scientific and rational approach cannot by nature access.

It can be observed that in the Roman Catholic world, from 1965 onwards, in the years following the Second Vatican Council (which caused a collapse of Christianity in the Western world[31]), theology has been "eaten up" by the human sciences, to the point that in the Catholic world, despite an attempt at recovery under the pontificates of Popes John Paul II and Benedict XVI, there are practically no real theologians left. This movement of absorption of theology by the human sciences had affected the Protestant world since the nineteenth century, in turn influencing the Catholic world. The danger today is that the Orthodox world will be influenced by both and be drawn into the same process of decadence.

The submission of theology to scientific or so-called scientific norms, its laicization and its secularization, linked to processes that we have previously mentioned, have had important repercussions on the teaching body itself. In academic institutions there has been a distrust of theologians who express in their work a confessional identity or simply manifest their faith. These have been systematically avoided in the recruiting processes, whatever their competence, the quality of their publications and their fame. In high-level university institutions such as, in France, the École Pratique des Hautes Etudes en Sciences Religieuses (EPHESR) or the Collège de France, where there are chairs clearly related to theological subjects such as "Byzantine Christianity" or "Orthodoxy," a candidate's declared or known adhesion to a Christian denomination is reason to block his/her recruitment. For many decades, the chairs relating to Christianity have in most cases been attributed to defrocked priests, whose distance from the Christian faith was well-known. The presentation of the Religious Sciences Section on the EPHESR website states: "The Religious Sciences section studies religious facts from a secular perspective." In the Faculties of Protestant Theology linked to the state (such as that of Strasbourg in France or those of Geneva and Lausanne in Switzerland), the same distance is required of teachers, and it is common to meet professors who not only question the essential data of the Christian faith (such as Christ's divinity, His virginal conception, His Resurrection, His Ascension, the resurrection of the dead, eternal life, paradise and hell, angels and demons, and the very notion of sin), but are downright agnostic and do not hesitate to declare themselves such. This was the case of one of the reference theologians of Protestantism, Professor Franz Camille Overbeck, who theorized about several of the points previously mentioned. He considered that any apologetic aim should be excluded from theology, that the Christianity elaborated by the Fathers of the Church had no relation to the Christianity taught by Christ and should therefore be banished. He considered knowledge and faith incompatible, and therefore considered that education, which favored the former, should exclude the latter. He believed that the only possible goal for a scientific theology was to build a secular history of the Church, well aware that such an enterprise could not serve to explain Christianity or even make it understood, but on the contrary ended in its destruction.

In Catholic theological faculties, the desire of teaching staff to distance themselves from the faith is less marked, but the concern to "scientificize" theological subjects has also affected the nature of teacher recruitment. Given the way theological subjects are conceived with a bias that gives them a scientific appearance, historians and linguists have been preferred for teaching subjects like biblical studies, patristics, and even dogmatics or liturgy. The human sciences have, since the 1960s, largely imposed themselves as references for the form and content of teaching, and therefore as an essential qualification criterion in the recruitment of teachers. Long before that, Protestantism had significantly impacted, in Catholic universities, the way of conceiving and teaching theological subjects, especially in the field of so-called biblical sciences.

Orthodox theological teaching establishments have been influenced by Catholicism and Protestantism, as can be observed in their organization (on similar lines to Catholic and Protestant theological faculties), and sometimes in the mode of teaching and its content. Since their origin and until today, many of their teachers have been trained in Catholic and Protestant theological faculties of Western Europe and have partly imported their methods. This influence has varied over time, depending on the subjects taught, and also according to the establishments and their status, whether or not they were integrated into a university and were close or not to other faculties with which they needed to align themselves organizationally, and on whether or not they were controlled by the state. The influence was often only relative, because Orthodox theological teaching establishments retained specific subjects that were absent or undervalued in similar Catholic or Protestant establishments. Also, many of their teachers were clerics, having parish activities and a liturgical and spiritual life which allowed them to keep a link with ecclesial realities and a theology lived out in its various expressions. These establishments also often remained under the control of the Church and subject to its specific needs.

However, the process of globalization which has affected the whole world since the last decades of the twentieth century (with a "noble" goal, in appearance, of openness and tolerance, but in reality with the underlying aim of removing, in all areas, the barriers that stand in the way of contemporary ultra-liberalism, the primary foundation and the ultimate goal of which are economic) has led to a certain leveling in this area as in others. This leveling has happened, not by a mix between the different "systems," which would have balanced out by virtue of a certain complementarity, but to the exclusive benefit of Western teaching methods. First because traditionally Orthodox countries remain generally fascinated by the West, which they take as a model and tend to imitate; second because, with the opening or abolition of borders, they have become more permeable to Western secular influences; third because these influences have powerful resources with which to spread and impose themselves; fourth because Western diplomas are more valued and recognized for access to professional careers; and fifth because the organization of the Western higher education system has become normative.

Faced with this process, fascinating in appearance but harmful in reality, the task of Orthodox theology must be to preserve its own identity, which cannot be reduced to that of profane or secular subjects, because Orthodox theology (in its broad sense) rests on other principles and aims at other, infinitely higher ends.

Chapter II

The Usefulness of Scientific Methods in Theology

In this study, we have no intention of denying the usefulness of scientific methods in theological studies; our goal is rather to point out their limits in relation to the different subjects. The word "limit" not being connotated negatively here, but designating the point up to which they have value (and specifying what this value is) and beyond which they no longer do (and specifying why).

It is known that in the field of research, which concerns specific branches of academic theology understood in the broad sense, certain scientific methods are not only useful but indispensable. It is also true that these methods have for the most part been defined and developed in the West in Catholic, Protestant, or Anglican university circles, and that Orthodox "university" circles have often remained less familiar with these methods, except where Orthodox teachers have been educated in Western faculties or research institutions where they have learned to use them. There has been and still is in the educational and research institutions of historically Orthodox countries, a certain lag compared to their Western counterparts. In recent years a number of efforts have sought to make up for this deficit, whether by sending students at the end of their studies to Western institutions for doctoral or postdoctoral studies, by inviting foreign professors to lecture or take part in colloquia, or by Orthodox researchers collaborating with

Western scientific journals, requiring adaptation to their standards, and self-training using Western works as models.

Before pointing to certain abuses or inadequacies in the application of these methods—or of some of them—to certain branches of Orthodox theology, it is appropriate to indicate which of them are useful and can be applied with profit to several areas.

1. Bibliographic Research

Bibliographic research is an essential prerequisite for any research because, in the scientific field, research consists in the exploration of subjects which have not yet been studied or which have been only partially studied. To establish this, it is first necessary to undertake a *status questionis* (status of the question), which can only be done by a careful study of the bibliography.

The bibliography then becomes a vital tool for the researcher to acquaint himself with the diversity of hypotheses, theses, comments, and interpretations, to confront his own views with them, to deepen his knowledge and understanding of his particular subject and, ultimately, to establish his own proposals on a firm basis.

Whatever subject one tackles, one is rarely the first to tackle it, and if one fails to take account of what has already been done, one finds oneself in the same situation as a physicist who ignores all scientific findings from previous centuries and starts his research from scratch. Not only would he be wasting his time, but the results of his own research would be weak (because lacking the intellectual capacity or requisite time to reconstitute all the knowledge acquired) and without interest (because he would only be repeating, in less depth, what we already know).

The bibliographical search must be as extensive as possible, that is, include all the studies carried out from the beginning throughout the world. This presupposes access to international bibliographical information resources, but also a good knowledge of the main official scientific languages in the field concerned—French, English, German, Italian—and the ability to handle other languages.

It is no longer possible today to confine oneself to one's own language (as too many researchers still do, particularly in English-speaking or in Slavic countries). In these circumstances, learning the main foreign research languages is an essential prerequisite. Currently, such learning is often organized, at least as far as English and French are concerned, in the Orthodox theological faculties in Russia and Romania, with Greece unfortunately lagging behind on this point, although this is partially compensated by the stays abroad of a certain number of students.

The bibliography must not, however, become an end in itself. I have observed that, in Russia especially, the quality of the scientific research is identified with the quantity of the bibliography. However, a bibliography must be qualitative rather than quantitative; it must be intelligent or, as it is more commonly said, "reasoned," that is to say well adapted to the study carried out and concentrated on it, otherwise one risks ending up with a work abounding in information but confused and lacking clear direction.

When an article provides precise bibliographical references in the footnotes, it is not only pointless but counterproductive to give a complete bibliography at the end of the article, as many Russian journals currently do in the belief that this makes them more scientific. If the notes indicate, as they should, the interesting passages used by citing the relevant pages of a book or article for which all the bibliographic references are provided,[32] the fact of giving in a final bibliography the list of articles or books in their entirety extends the references beyond what the author has precisely in mind, and losing the forest for the trees.

2. The Critical Editions of Texts (Biblical, Patristic, Hagiographic, Canonical, etc.) and Their Use

One of the main contributions of the application of scientific methods to theological subjects has been and remains the critical edition of the original texts used in the biblical, patristic, hagiographic, and liturgical fields.

This work has been done since the eighteenth centuries and continues in the Protestant and Catholic world especially, where reference collections such as "Sources chrétiennes," the "Collection des Universités de France," the "Corpus Christianorum" ("Series Latina" and "Series Graeca"), the "Corpus Scriptorum Christianorum Orientalium," the "Analecta Bollandiana," etc. provide students and researchers across the world with reliable texts. It is obviously these texts which absolutely must serve as references for all studies carried out concerning their content, without the need to mention the serious, but unscientific, older editions like the "Patrologia Graeca" or the "Patrologia Latina" other than as a reminder when they exist. It is important to specify this, because too many students in Orthodox countries are still working with translations, based on poorly outdated editions.

The Orthodox countries have participated very modestly in the work of publishing ancient original texts (although in Greece there have been quality editions of the complete works of Gregory Palamas and of some late Byzantine authors), but they benefit greatly from the work done in Western Europe.

One is right to insist, however, that in earlier centuries in the Orthodox world, an effort was already made to publish quality editions based on the comparison of various manuscripts, particularly in the edition of the Greek *Philokalia* composed by Nicodemus the Hagiorite and Macarius of Corinth, and that of the Slavonic *Philokalia* by Paisius Velitchkovsky. It should be noted that there is also a wide field of possibilities—which have begun to be exploited—to publish locally with scientific standards the ancient authors that have been ignored by Western publishing programs.

Notable efforts have also been made for several years in Russia, Greece, and Romania to publish quality translations from the critical reference editions, and to accompany them with equally high-quality introductions and annotations.

Any critical edition, being the result of a highly technical process which also requires a perfect knowledge of the ancient languages involved, obviously requires specialized training. As such it appeals primarily to philologists, however, it is only fully effective when these scholars also have theological training in the field concerned (biblical, patristic, hagiographic, liturgical, etc.). This is valuable for a good understanding of the text but also for the quality of the introductions and annotations, although often—and this is the optimal solution—these are entrusted to specialists working in close collaboration with the editors.

However, introductions and annotations must always be read with a certain critical distance, because it is not uncommon for committed authors to give tendentious interpretations.[33]

3. Historical Criticism

Scientific methods in the field of history were developed in the nineteenth century. They consist mainly of the two forms of criticism to which the sources are subjected, and which aim to ensure their authenticity and the truth of their content: external criticism (which relates to their form: dating, author, etc.) and internal criticism which relates to their content (internal consistency, faithfulness to the facts, truth of the testimony, etc.). This requires the searching for, comparison and evaluation of diverse sources.

Once the sources have been established, they should be respected, both in order to define a hypothesis and to verify it. The human sciences, of which history is a part, generally following the same approach here as the physical or natural sciences, however for history, an experimental verification is impossible because it consists of what are by nature past, unique, and non-reproducible facts.

However as modern historians (freed from the illusions of nineteenth-century positivist historians) have emphasized, recourse to facts alone does not make for objective history. These facts must be ordered, implying a degree of subjectivity on the part of the historian. This subjectivity also intervenes in the determination of causes: these are always multiple and complex, because even one-off events that appear to be immediate causes are linked to a political, economic, social context, and to more distant causes. Finally, and above all, subjectivity intervenes in interpretation. Indeed, the facts often lend themselves to a multitude of—also potentially aberrant—interpretations.

We will see the problems this poses when it comes to the history of the Church; but with regard to its starting point, the verification of sources, this can only benefit from the application of scientific methods. The same is true of hagiography, although in this area too special problems arise, which we will examine later.

4. The Use of References (Precise and Exact)

The Fathers often quoted their predecessors and even biblical texts from memory and approximately, without quotation marks and without references, as is still practiced today among preachers, who generally improvise their sermons. It is also the practice of a certain number of Orthodox authors, who act in this way because they have always done so, or out of laziness, or out of a desire to reformulate quotations in accordance with their subject or their style (if not their own ideas!).

The methodology which is essential today everywhere in the various fields of theological studies where references and quotations are brought into play requires not only the respect of the sources as we said previously, but also exact quotations, placed in quotation marks, and precise, exact references, which will not only serve to justify the writer's arguments, but will allow readers to immediately find the quoted text, either to verify its accuracy if they have any doubts, or to learn about its context, which is often decisive for its meaning. The references must be those of the original text (Greek, Latin, Hebrew, Coptic, Syriac, etc.) in its critical edition, the reference to the translation not necessarily being given in second place, but always in the bibliography, subject to any modifications that may legitimately be made to it.

5. Rational Argument

Even if theology is not, like philosophy, a totally rational subject, argumentation plays a certain role in it. In theological works, it is necessary not only to give precise references to the texts and works evoked, but to give a precise justification to what one affirms, because here again a certain number of students tend, as we do it in preaching, to affirm without justifying.

Argumentation (necessarily rational and using the rules of logic) is particularly necessary when dealing with controversial subjects, and when one needs to criticize someone else's foreign interpretation deemed false or inaccurate, and firmly establish one's own interpretation.

Although modern science gives an essential place to the processes of reasoning and rational argumentation, the use of these where applicable in the fields of theology is not a recent phenomenon, appearing only under the influence of the scientific methodology which has come into being over the last three centuries. Already the Apologists of the first centuries applied them against the pagan philosophies which they criticized. These processes occupied a major place in the refutation of heresies by all the Fathers (we can see them at work in particular in the refutation of Eunomius and his disciples by Basil the Great and Gregory of Nyssa, or in the refutation of Monoenergism and monotheletism by Maximus the Confessor), who were forced to confront the complex arguments of their adversaries. A further step was taken when, in the controversies over the Filioque, the Eastern Fathers had to face the very precise rational methods of argumentation of the scholastic theologians. We see it for example in a characteristic way in the various treatises of Gregory of Cyprus,[34] or in Nilus

Cabasilas in his treatise *On the Holy Spirit*,[35] both of whom adapted their methods of argumentation to that of their adversaries. Between the two, St Gregory Palamas, in his *Demonstrative Treatises on the Procession of the Holy Spirit*, defended against Barlaam the legitimacy of demonstration in theology.[36]

Rational argumentation is therefore intimately linked, from the outset, to apologetics, which is an essential dimension of theology as we have underlined previously.

Chapter III

Dogmatic Theology

A large part of the discussion in the first chapter concerned dogmatic theology, the queen of theological disciplines. The present chapter will therefore only provide some complementary items linked explicitly to dogmatic theology in the context of the multiplication of theological subjects.

Dogmatic theology is the study of dogma (i.e., the content of the faith of the Church) in its various components.

It is a thematic study, but it nevertheless appeals to history, because dogma was clarified and formulated progressively—that is, with ever greater precision—especially over the course of the first eight centuries. Because dogma is based on Revelation, the basis of which is Holy Scripture, dogmatic theology appeals to biblical studies; because it was defined by the Councils, it appeals to the history of the Councils; because it was elaborated by the Fathers of the Church, it necessarily appeals to patrology (here we find again the need to combine the different subjects of theological education).

However, being a systematic study, it must therefore offer syntheses of all the themes studied, and in this it goes beyond the fragmentation inherent in biblical studies, in history or in patrology.

1. The first component of dogmatic theology is the doctrine of the Trinity, because God is Trinity, and it is the Trinitarian doctrine which, in the history of the Church, gave rise to the first controversies and

therefore was the first dogma to be defined. This took place especially during the fourth century with, first, the affirmation of God as being three hypostases (or persons) and a single nature (or essence); second, the affirmation of the divinity of Christ; and third, the affirmation of the divinity of the Holy Spirit. However, the appearance in the West of the Filioque and its doctrinal formalization by Roman Catholicism gave rise to new controversies and new clarifications concerning the relationship of the three divine Persons to each other and concerning their common nature (notably in the ninth, thirteenth, and fourteenth centuries).

Linked to the question of God is the theology of divine energies, present from the origins in the Tradition of the Christian East,[37] but to which St Gregory Palamas gave in the fourteenth century a maximum of explanation and precision. The controversies aroused by this theology on the part of Roman Catholicism and some Byzantine theologians, influenced on the one hand by humanism and on the other by the Latin tradition—controversies which still persist today—require that it be the subject of careful and in-depth study, given also its essential implications in the field of Orthodox spirituality.[38]

2. The second component of dogmatic theology is Christology, which was partly (concerning the divinity of Christ) defined in the framework of the Trinitarian controversies of the fourth century, and for partly (concerning the natures and the hypostasis of Christ) in the framework of the controversies aroused in the fifth and sixth centuries by Nestorianism and monophysitism, and in the seventh century by monoenergism and monotheletism. The study of these questions is important not only in the framework of basic theological training, but also in the framework of the current ongoing dialogue with non-Chalcedonian Churches.

3. A third component of dogmatic theology is soteriology (doctrine of salvation) which is obviously closely related to Christology but corresponds to a different perspective from the previous one

because it is concerned, not with the natures and the person of Christ considered in themselves, but with His various acts to accomplish the salvation of men—what is called His "Saving Economy"—with a view to their deification.

4. Because the salvation and deification of men is accomplished in the Church, the Body of Christ, the fourth component of dogmatic theology is ecclesiology (in its properly dogmatic dimension, and not in its institutional dimension).

5. Because salvation and deification find their fulfillment (full realization) at the end of time and in the Kingdom of Heaven, the fifth component of dogmatic theology is eschatology, the doctrine of the last things.

We see that this order is that of the Creed, with dogmatic theology including moreover the study of the different Confessions of faith which summarize the dogma.

We can obviously attach to dogmatic theology other matters which have been the subject of dogmatic definitions during Councils: for example iconology in its properly dogmatic component, which was the subject of the Council of Nicaea II, although it is more logical to attach this component to iconology taken as a whole where this constitutes, within the framework of theological studies, an independent subject.

We can also attach to dogmatic theology cosmology, angelology, demonology, and Mariology, because these subjects are rarely studied as independent entities, and would not otherwise be approached.

But the five themes listed above are more than enough to occupy teaching in all study cycles: they are extremely vast and complex, and their assimilation calls for much application, time, and maturity. Alas, we observe that students' training is almost always insufficient at the end of their studies. In discussions with students following lectures I have given in theological academies or faculties of theology in various Orthodox countries, I have often been surprised by the questions that have been put to me and which revealed that essential points of dogma, particularly in the areas of triadology and Christology, have not been understood (e.g., with regard to the nature and relationships of the essence and hypostases of the Trinity, or of the natures and hypostasis of Christ). I have had the same impression when reading certain articles or seeing certain productions of former theology students and even professors, where gross errors were made, which showed that elementary principles had not been assimilated. The understanding of Triadology and Christology requires, in fact, a long and deep labor, in particular a long exposure to the Fathers who worked it out.

It is this fundamental work that dogmatic theology must set about, it is on these bases that it must concentrate.

The difference between dogmatic theology in an Orthodox context and dogmatic theology in a Roman Catholic or Protestant context is that the former gives essential importance to the foundations of dogmatic theology as found in the Councils, in the Fathers, and in the creeds of the Orthodox Church, while the latter is more interested in, and often accords priority to, later authors whose personal dogmatic constructions are powerful (like that of Thomas Aquinas in Roman Catholicism) or modern (like those of Tillich or Pannenberg in Protestantism), but which, of course, from the Orthodox point of view, depart from Tradition. These tendencies of the Western confessions are moreover linked to two positions foreign to Orthodox theology: the Roman Catholic conception of a progress of dogma which allows for innovations, and the Protestant rejection of the patristic tradition which makes the development of the theology which it considers to be true to start at the time of the Reformation. Moreover, the secularization undergone by these two Christian denominations in the twentieth century tends to make them give preference to modern theologians, while Orthodoxy is deeply attached to the Fathers of theology, who formulated the dogmas in a sufficiently complete form to confer on the content of the faith the maximum possible precision.

Among them, traditional Orthodox teaching favors those Fathers who contributed most to explaining and clarifying the Orthodox faith, such as Sts. Athanasius of Alexandria, Basil of Caesarea, Gregory the Theologian, Gregory of Nyssa, Maximus the Confessor, Photios the Great, and Gregory Palamas. The study of St John Damascene, who elaborated a remarkable synthesis, ought also to occupy a central place.

The idea that Orthodox dogmatic theology is therefore backward-looking and not adapted to the modern world is not correct because, as we have said, the Fathers had a discourse based on the Gospel, on their life in the Church, and on their personal spiritual experience, and this discourse is part of the catholic Tradition of the Church which transcends the limits of time. It has, because of this, a living and universal character which makes it timeless and always current. On the contrary, what is modern is quickly outdated, quickly becomes obsolete, especially in the framework of the Western theology which developed in the second half of the twentieth century and which aims to be "contextual," i.e., linked to the particular circumstances of a historical moment, a particular social context or a specific group.[39] This is confirmed today by the fact that the great Catholic and Protestant theologians who were in vogue in the middle of the twentieth century hardly arouse interest anymore in the West itself.

It would be a mistake for Orthodox theological teaching and practice to engage in the study of these theologies and to seek to give to dogmatic theology new developments inspired by their problems or their themes. The current interest of some Orthodox theologians (in particular Greeks, Americans, and Russians, to tell the truth very much a minority and marginal) in the currents of Protestant theology and especially Roman Catholic theology (known as "new theology") of the mid-twentieth century,[40] as well as in the more recent current of "Radical Orthodoxy"[41] does not make sense and constitutes a waste of time, for the reason that these currents aim to settle problems internal to Western theology (due to its deviationist past which goes back at least to scholasticism) which have remained foreign to Orthodoxy.[42] The only value in taking an interest in them would be to show how traditional Orthodox theology has long solved the problems they face and avoided the contradictions and impasses with which they find themselves confronted.

Chapter IV

Sacred Scripture and Its Exegesis

1. The Status of Sacred Scripture in the Orthodox Tradition

It is generally considered among Christians that Holy Scripture is the basis of all theology (in the broad sense) because it is the primary expression of Revelation. The Old Testament contains, through the words of Moses and the prophets, the initial Revelation of God, the first expression of His will and His promises. The New Testament reveals the direction and significance of the Old Testament. It not only introduces us to the earthly life of Christ, the Incarnate Word, but transmits to us His words which, given their full meaning by the action of the Holy Spirit, bring us the fullness of Revelation. The epistles of Sts, Paul, Peter, James, and John are expositions of the teaching of Christ by persons who received this directly by living with him (the latter three) or indirectly by personal revelation (St Paul).

For Protestantism, the Bible is self-sufficient, which Luther expressed by the principle *sola scriptura*. This means that it is the supreme reference, the sole and ultimate authority in the fields of faith and Christian life. This implies that there is no obligatory and authorized intermediary between the Scripture itself and the person of the faithful, who can interpret it freely (what Protestantism calls "the spirit of free examination").

Roman Catholicism has a radically different position: the Bible must be understood through the filter of what it calls "the magisterium," that is, the hierarchy of the Church headed by the Pope.

The conception of the Orthodox Church differs from the previous two on several levels. A close relationship is established in several ways between Scripture and Tradition. First of all, Scripture is an element of Tradition, and as such cannot be properly understood outside of it, or in other words it has no autonomy. On the one hand, Tradition existed before Scripture: Scripture is the recording in writing of facts and words concerning Christ and His disciples which were first transmitted verbally (in other words by an oral tradition). On the other hand, Scripture, once recorded, requires interpretation. It cannot, therefore, be subject to the judgment of individuals, as Protestants believe, because that inevitably gives rise to not only diverse but contradictory and incompatible interpretations (as can be observed between the different Protestant denominations and within each of them between the different faithful). Indeed, the text lends itself by its often-ambiguous, symbolic, or polysemic character to a multitude of interpretations, some of which are legitimate and others not, the distinction between the latter and the former requiring the use of a criterion external to Scripture itself and to the multiplicity of individual readers. This requirement is confirmed and reinforced by the fact that multiple sects, including very aberrant ones, find justifications in their own interpretations of Scripture, as have the multiple heresies of the past. The Roman Catholic conception that makes the interpretation of Scripture depend on the magisterium is legitimate (providing one includes in this notion the bishops and not only or not primarily the pope), but not sufficient. It is legitimate insofar as, very early on, in the Church, the interpretation of the Scriptures was an attribute of the episcopate, which is justified by the fact that the episcopal ministry is considered to be the continuity of the apostolic ministry (the bishops are the successors of the Apostles, to whom is entrusted by Christ the mission of teaching all nations. This is why catechesis was also an attribute of the episcopal ministry). This understanding is not sufficient because, according to the Orthodox Church, truth is an attribute of the entire body of Christ which is its depositary and transmits it from generation to generation in a living way, in what is called Tradition. Tradition includes the kerygma (apostolic preaching), which is its basis, but also the exegesis of the Fathers of the Church of all times in their sermons, their written commentaries, or in what they ruled in the Councils in which they participated. It also includes the interpretation the Church gives of Scripture in its liturgical services, or in a living and varied way by means of the homilies of the clerics (bishops, and priests who are their delegates and representatives), or in a fixed and unequivocal way by means of the *paremias,* that is extracts from the Old Testament, the meaning of which (in particular typological—see below) relates to the liturgical feasts for which they are prescribed. We therefore understand that Scripture, for the Orthodox Church, takes on its meaning only within a global ecclesial context, in other words, Catholic in the etymological sense of this term: "according to the whole."

We therefore see that, in theological studies, Holy Scripture and its interpretation as subjects of teaching and learning, or at a higher level, as objects of scientific study, cannot be separated, isolated, and studied independently of an ecclesial context. It requires that the approach specific to the Church be respected, in which the reference to the Fathers plays a major role, and where the ecclesial use of the biblical texts and their spiritual purpose must be taken into account.

2. The Damaging Character of Modern Protestant and Catholic Exegesis

a. The Limits of Textual Criticism

Protestant biblical studies and Roman Catholic biblical studies (which in fact took their model from them) are essentially historical-philological in nature. A similar method is found also in other fields of theological studies (including patrology) but in the case of biblical studies this method takes a more radical form than elsewhere.

The biblical texts are treated—as scientific methodology requires—as ordinary literary texts, enjoying no particular authority, either intrinsic or attributed by Tradition, and therefore totally open to critical investigation.

More than the spiritual meaning of the texts of Sacred Scripture (which the Orthodox tradition considers essential), it is the literary form of the texts—their syntactic and lexical character—which is the primary focus of attention, and on this basis the identity of the speaker and the social and historical context are deemed to have determined the form and meaning of his speech.[43] It often happens that these studies reveal the texts as assemblages of various sources (including "pagan"), with various layers, various redactions, and therefore multiple authors.

This method applies to the texts of the Old Testament and the New Testament. It has the effect of dissolving the unity of the texts, the identity of their authors, and consequently their authority. Applied to the Epistles of St Paul, it results in establishing a distinction between the Pauline Epistles and the pseudo-Pauline Epistles, the latter having undetermined authors and acquiring the dubious status of apocryphal texts. Applied to the Gospels, and emphasizing that their writing was carried out several decades after the earthly life of Christ, it removes in several cases the authorship of the apostle-evangelists who were witnesses of the life of Christ and hearers of His words. It highlights the probable losses and alterations due both to the oral transmission which preceded the written record and to the change of language (from Aramaic, the language spoken by Christ, to Greek, the language of the Gospels); it highlights the possible multiplicity of sources; it emphasizes the diversity and heterogeneity of the writing of the four Gospels, and results in the accounts of the episodes of the life of Christ and the acts accomplished by Him losing their authority, as well His words, noting that these are attributed to Him only in a relative and uncertain way. Some biblical scholars even go so far as to affirm that there is no single word in the Gospels that can be attributed with certainty to Christ Himself.

This way of studying the Scriptures, which completely relativizes its content, has greatly contributed to developing within Protestantism and Catholicism, at least among those who have been trained in such a method of approaching the Scriptures, the secularization from which these two denominations suffer very strongly today, and the agnosticism which affects part of their elites, especially in Protestantism (professors of faculties of theology, educated theologians and clerics, etc.).

b. Decentering from the Canon and Interest in Apocryphal Writings

The fact that in the critical approach part of the texts of the Old Testament and the New Testament acquire the status of apocryphal writings gives the apocryphal writings a status equivalent to the canonical texts, and ascribes equal value to them. Hence the considerable growth in the interest accorded to the apocryphal writings in Protestant biblical studies, to the extent even of taking precedence over the canonical texts, and of conferring on apocryphal specialists an added value in recruitment to university teaching positions in disciplines other than biblical studies. For example, for several decades, at the Faculty of Protestant Theology in Strasbourg, the positions of lecturers and professors of "History of Ancient Christianity" (a subject which in fact covers patrology) have been recruited mainly from specialists in the edition of apocryphal texts. This tendency has unfortunately contaminated other fields, since in certain faculties or academies of Orthodox theology, as I noted in a previous chapter, the study of apocryphal texts of Church Fathers or often heterodox marginal authors has taken its place alongside the study of the Orthodox Fathers and their authentic texts and has become for teachers a way of enhancing their images by testifying to their having trained in the "scientific" methods of the West.

One can give as an argument, to justify study of the apocryphal writings, that the canon of the Scriptures took a certain time to be defined, and that the hesitation to which this testifies gives it a certain relativity. But what must be recognized today, in the framework of theological studies, is what the Church has once and for all defined at a certain point. This is what should occupy the full attention of biblical studies, because there is already enough to do to know the books included in the canon without dispersing one's energies on the others, often to the detriment of the first. There are of course a few exceptions to this: almost all the episodes from the Life of the Mother of God—which occupy an important place in the liturgical services of the Orthodox Church and in her iconography (a program of frescoes is dedicated to her in many churches)—are known to us only from apocryphal texts (in the first place the *Proto-Gospel of James* and the *Greek Dormition of Pseudo John*) which it is therefore useful to know. But there again "the exception confirms the rule": the object of study must be circumscribed in relation to what the Church has integrated and currently endorses, not only by recognizing a precise list of sacred texts constituting the canon of Scripture, and also, at their level, the texts on which it relies in its traditional liturgical or iconographic practice.

c. The Excesses of Historicism

Owing in particular to the concern to give a scientific character to biblical studies—often called "Biblical Sciences"—out of a desire to "scientificize" theological studies in general (for reasons as diverse as the secularization of Western Christian denominations or the concern to give theological studies a university status equivalent to that of other university subjects dominated by the methodology of the "human sciences")—very great importance has been accorded, in Protestantism and in Catholicism, to the historical approach to biblical texts, to the point where what is called "historicism" dominates.[44] This has become, along with the philological approach, which too has taken excessive proportions, the almost exclusive principle of biblical exegesis. Texts are commented on and understood based on their historical dating, and therefore also their historical (political and sociocultural) context. Ultimately, in this way, they are perceived as the products of a historical moment, which determines their form and content, at the expense of spiritual interpretation.

However, for the Orthodox Tradition, as expressed particularly in the writings of the Fathers, both ancient and contemporary, and in the liturgical services, it is this spiritual interpretation which is essential. For this spiritual interpretation, it does not really matter who is the author of the texts, or at what time and in what context they were written. Biblical texts are considered to be inspired by God (who is therefore their true author, even if He expresses Himself in this case through human words borrowed from a particular language) and as having a universal scope in space and in time. The Fathers who commented on the Scriptures, even when dealing with very specific historical events, always strove, according to their exegetical method (which we will explain below) to find in them a symbolic or typological meaning which transcends them. The history of God's chosen people in the Old Testament must of course be known and studied, but this must be done in the framework of history courses (with the help of biblical texts) rather than in the framework of Bible studies themselves, where not only every book of the Bible, but every verse in every book has meaning and value on its own.

Let us add that the historical approach to the texts is often disappointing, posing more problems than it solves: the dates of composition are often uncertain and at times vary by several centuries, the authors are often poorly identified, and the purpose of the texts, in some cases, does not appear clearly. This blurs more than it clarifies the approach to the texts.

A typical example is the *Song of Songs* which, from this point of view, produces difficulties and uncertainties:

– the range of dates proposed for its writing is very wide, extending from the tenth to the first century BC;

– although the text is in the first verse attributed to Solomon and therefore appears as in the Bible among the Wisdom books, we do not really know who is the author, or even if this is a man or a woman (the second hypothesis is supported by some scholars);

– we are not sure that the text is a whole: some think that what we have is a collection of love songs—with a strong erotic dimension—to which an editor has attempted to give unity by using keywords;

– it is not sure that the whole follows an overall plan (some Bible scholars see it as a succession of small units with no apparent link);

– both ancient and modern commentators cannot agree on the number of speakers and on the exact distribution of responses (it is often very difficult to know who is speaking);

– the overall meaning is not clear: as the name of God never appears, some commentators see it as "the least biblical of the books of the Bible" and note that it could be a profane love song (celebrating and justifying, according to some, an idyll between Solomon and one of his concubines, perhaps Pharaoh's daughter).

The *Song of Songs* has been the subject of commentary by several Church Fathers, in particular Origen and Gregory of Nyssa. We note that these Fathers paid no attention to the preceding questions—which on the other hand hold all the attention of the modern scientific approach, although completely sterile for the Christian life—but immediately tackled the text from the spiritual viewpoint, seeing in it an allegory of the wedding of the Church and of Christ, or of the union of the soul with God. It is rather these kinds of interpretations that should hold the attention of Orthodox studies of the text.

Let us take another example: that of the Psalms of David. The historical/contextual approach seeks to relate the psalms, in which there is often talk of fighting against enemies, to the wars waged by King David. A correlative psychological approach sees in a certain number of passages, on the one hand, paranoid symptoms and on the other hand symptoms of depression. The recurring feelings of guilt linked to the evocation of sins are related to David's various faults (specifically murder and adultery, perhaps rape according to certain biblical scholars concerning his meeting with Bathsheba . . .).

The psalms have been a major component of prayers and liturgical offices since the origin of Christianity. In this usage, the historical context of their composition plays no role. Each believer takes the words in the way he chooses and adapts them to his own situation. How can this be done? This is what the Fathers of the Church explain in their commentaries on the Psalms, again by bringing out their allegorical and symbolic meanings. The main role of biblical studies is to train students to understand these spiritual meanings. This brings about a total change of perspective compared to the "biblical sciences" of the Western denominations, because what is privileged is not an abstract knowledge which creates a distance between the reader and the text, but a spiritual knowledge that allows him to appropriate the latter in accordance with its true purpose in the context of ecclesial and personal prayer.

We see how, in this perspective, biblical studies cannot be considered as an autonomous subject, but must be developed in close relationship with liturgical theology, ascetic theology, and patrology. This makes it possible to understand what the passions are, to which all the passages of the psalms that mention "my enemies" refer, together with sins and demons. This also helps to understand that the verses, "O daughter of Babylon, thou cursed one, blessed shall he be that shall do unto thee, as thou hast done unto us. Blessed is he that shall seize and dash thine infants against a rock" (Ps 136: 8–9) do not refer to the city of Babylon as such and do not concern revenge against the descendants of its inhabitants, but that the little children of Babylon are evil thoughts (which the Greek Fathers call *logismoi*) whom the faithful must kill at birth in mind and heart, by means of the invocation of the Name of Jesus ("the Rock"), so that they do not grow to become uncontrollable and serve as food to the passions.

d. The Decoupling of the Old Testament from the New Testament

As we have already said, one effect of the specialization of theological subjects is their fragmentation, which in several areas leads us to lose sight of their fundamental interconnectedness. In biblical studies, it is customary to separate the study of the Old Testament and that of the New Testament into two subjects, each with its own specialist teacher or teachers. This leads to the situation in which each of the two parts of the Bible is studied for itself, independently of the other. The negative effects of this dissociation are felt especially in the study of the Old Testament. From the Orthodox perspective, which corresponds to the patristic perspective but also to the liturgical one (i.e., to say the way in which the texts are integrated and perceived in the framework of liturgical services), the Old Testament has no significance by itself, but only in relation to and through the New Testament, of which its narratives are a preparation, an announcement, a prefiguration. This appears particularly clearly in the "paremias" (biblical passages) of the Vespers of the feasts which celebrate the great stages of the saving economy of the Incarnate Word, where the texts, selected from different books of the Old Testament, all point toward these "stages," announcing and prefiguring them in a more or less clear, more or less symbolic way. This typological understanding of the Old Testament is also that of the Fathers in their exegetical works, which at times also give a moral or spiritual interpretation of certain passages, but always in the light of Christianity and its New Testament foundation. All agree with St Augustine's famous formula: "*Novum Testamentum in Vetere latet. Vetus Testamentum in Novo patet*" (The New Testament is hidden in the Old. The Old Testament is revealed in the New).[45] The interpretation of the Old Testament taken on its own gives rise to a Hebrew interpretation which, of course, is fully justified in the framework of Judaism, but not in that of Christianity.

e. Hebraism: Only of Relative Interest. The Septuagint as a Reference Text

However, Protestantism has favored such Hebraicizing interpretation, followed in part by modern-day Catholicism. This interpretation has been reinforced by the importance given, in correlation with biblical studies, to the learning of Hebrew, and by the philological study of the Bible based on the Hebrew text, which served as a reference for St Jerome's Latin translation—the Vulgate—and was made the official text of the Bible for Latin Christianity (although for a time a number of Latin Fathers continued to refer to the Greek text).

For the Orthodox study of the Old Testament, the study of the Hebrew text and the Hebrew language is only of relative interest, since the reference text for the Greek Fathers and for the Orthodox Church is the Greek text of the Septuagint.[46] This text is not only a translation, but often also an interpretation of the Hebrew text with its own logic and coherence. It is knowledge of Greek that is required for its study of this text, that is situated in a "Hellenic ambience" very different from the "Hebraic ambience" and in any case far removed from the rabbinic interpretations to which Protestantism and Catholicism accord great importance, often reinforced by the contemporary preoccupation with interreligious dialogue.

Father Georges Florovsky strongly opposed the Hebraicizing of biblical studies that he saw in Protestantism from the nineteenth century onwards and which Catholicism had adopted in the twentieth century. On the one hand, he aptly pointed out that in Christianity "the categories of priestly Hebraicism have lost their independent meaning, and [that] any attempt to separate or detach them from the totality of the Christian synthesis can produce only a relapse into Judaism," and that "the truth of 'Hebraism' is already incorporated into the Hellenic synthesis, for Hellenism has become part of the Church, precisely thanks to a biblical grafting."[47] On the other hand, agreeing with what we have said previously, he notes that according to the conception and practice of the Orthodox Church (confirmed by the liturgical use of the texts of the Old Testament and by the exegetical method of the Fathers), it is the New Testament that is the key to interpreting the Old. For him, the revival of Hebraicism testifies to an inability to read the Bible with the Church. All Jewish claims to a correct interpretation of the Old Testament, he says, "must be formally rejected," for "the Old Testament no longer belongs to the Jews, it belongs to the Church alone," which is "the only Israel of God." "Only the Church of Christ keeps now the right key to the Scriptures, the true key to the prophecies of old. Because all these prophecies are fulfilled in Christ." "New light has been thrown on the old revelations by Him who came just to accomplish and to fulfil the Law and the Prophets. [...]. Christ Jesus is the Alpha and Omega of the Scriptures, both the climax and knot of the Bible."[48]

f. Two Major Damaging Effects of Western Historical-philological Methodology: The Decomposition of Scripture and the Discrediting and Destruction of Its Authority

If we recapitulate the disadvantages, from an Orthodox point of view, of the method previously described, we can first of all note that Sacred Scripture, when studied in itself and for itself, finds itself isolated from the ecclesial context which gives it its meaning. It also loses the spiritual purpose which is essential to it, both in its "liturgical" reading in the framework of the church and in the "private" reading of the faithful. Both the historical approach and by the pure philological approach have the effect of decomposing the texts of Scripture to the extreme. They become like an automobile which has been dismantled into its constituent parts, which loses its overall structure and can no longer be driven, or like a flower from which the petals and stamens have been removed and separated, and which has lost its beauty and its scent. Another effect of this method is to treat the sacred texts as profane texts, the inspiration of which is not divine but human, and the bases of which are not spiritual but psychological and sociocultural. The highlighting of a multitude of uncertainties concerning their dating, their authorship, and their origin is added to the previous elements to relativize them and remove their authority. This is further accentuated when the texts are subjected to openly desacralizing, secularizing, and devaluing interpretative ideologies advocated and applied by openly agnostic exegetes, such as the "demythologization" elaborated by the Lutheran theologian Rudolph Bultmann, which still strongly marks current exegesis, in the first place Protestant, but also Roman Catholic. Bultmann saw demythologization as a reinterpretation to make the Gospel acceptable and understandable to contemporary man, out of a desire to adapt to the supposed needs of modern man that was also one of the main projects of the Second Vatican Council. We have seen, in the decadence of Western Christian denominations since the time of this Council,[49] that this project failed and that this conception was totally counterproductive.

We have met many Orthodox students who, having come to pursue their studies in Catholic or Protestant theology faculties in Western Europe, have been extremely surprised and even shocked by the total disconnection of biblical studies from the spiritual meaning of Scripture, and even more by the concern to discredit the Christian faith even on essential points (the Trinity, the divinity of Christ, His virginal conception, His miracles, His Resurrection, His Ascension, His real presence in the Eucharist, life after death, Paradise and hell, angels and demons, sin, etc.).

3. Principles of Orthodox Exegesis

The preceding remarks have brought to the surface the problems posed by Catholic and Protestant biblical studies to the Orthodox understanding of Sacred Scripture. Let us recall the main principles of the Orthodox approach here.

a. The Authority of Scripture

The texts of the Old and New Testaments are no ordinary literary texts. Although located historically in particular sociocultural contexts and emanating from authors having their own personalities, they are texts inspired by God, constituting a *Sacred* Scripture, having a sacred character and a universal value beyond their particular historical significance. As such, they possess a value and an authority which demand respect. This respect is manifested by the Church in the solemn way in which she carries the books containing them, in the way she proclaims them through consecrated readers (ordained readers, subdeacons, deacons, priests) during liturgical services, and also by the attribution of the tasks of commenting on them to the bishop and his delegates and representatives, the priests.

b. "Scriptura non sola": The Integration of Scripture into the Church and Its Tradition

Scripture cannot be understood and interpreted on its own. The Orthodox Church therefore does not accept the basic Protestant principle of *sola scriptura*. Scripture needs to be interpreted, and among the multiplicity of possible *a priori* interpretations calls for a correct one. Its correct interpretation does not depend on each individual (as in Protestantism which admits the "principle of free examination") nor on the magisterium alone (as in Roman Catholicism), but on the Church as a whole (in its catholicity), within the framework of Tradition. Tradition is represented by the Fathers of the Church (whose mode of approach to Scripture and exegesis are inescapable references), by the liturgical offices (which in the choice of the biblical texts which are appropriate to them contribute to defining their meaning), and by those persons who, in an ever current and living way, are specially authorized, within the Church, in the context of liturgical life and for the faithful, to comment on the Scriptures: the bishops and the priests who are their delegates. This does not mean that, in the context of biblical studies, teachers must necessarily be bishops or priests, but it does imply that they must in all cases reflect in their teaching the essential understanding of the relationship of Scripture to Tradition as a whole, and especially to the Fathers of the Church who are in this case an essential element.

c. The Indissoluble Bond of the Old Testament with the New Testament. The Fundamentally Typological Character of the Old Testament

Another basic principle of the Orthodox approach is that the study of the Old Testament cannot be separated from that of the New Testament, since in Christianity the Old Testament has no value and meaning by itself but only takes these on through the New Testament, as a preparation for and an announcement of what the latter relates. For this reason the Old Testament requires, for a large number of texts, a typological interpretation, and for others a symbolic interpretation, the knowledge of the historical facts themselves being of secondary interest, as confirmed by the fact that these are ignored in both liturgical and private spiritual use.

d. The Patristic Foundations of Orthodox Exegesis. Forms and Levels of Interpretation

The Fathers, who taken as a whole are one of the major constituents of Tradition, developed a method of interpreting the Scriptures which remains a model. This method promotes different levels of interpretation that go way beyond the historical and literal interpretations favored in modern times by the approach adopted by Western Christian denominations.

It is usual, at the academic level, to distinguish between two schools or exegetical currents among the Fathers. These are the Antiochian school and the Alexandrian school, the first practicing a literal exegesis, the second a symbolic (or allegorical) exegesis. In fact, the distinction is less clear-cut, because the representatives of the Antiochian school (to which St John Chrysostom, for example, is attached) are far from exclusively literalist and give a lot of room to the symbolic meaning, while those of the Alexandrian school (with Origen as its prototype) are far from neglecting the literal meaning of the texts. It can be said that all the Fathers interpret the Scriptures on multiple levels, even if some manifest a more developed taste or talent for this or that type, and consequently the degree of "literalism" or "symbolism" varies in their respective works.

It is astonishing that Western Christianity, which in modern times has overwhelmingly favored the literal and historical approaches in its exegetical methods, had for many centuries (until a decadence sets in from the Renaissance onwards), defined in the most precise way four levels at which the Scriptures can be read, and therefore four levels of interpretation: (1) the literal meaning (also called the historical meaning, although it is broader than this); (2) the allegorical meaning (which includes the typological meaning); (3) the tropological (also called moral) meaning; (4) the anagogic meaning (from the Greek word *anagoge* which in Greek means "ascent") because this meaning elevates the soul toward the divine, which is the highest and the least evident way of reading.

It was St John Cassian (360–435) who provided an interface between the East and the West, who for the first time distinguished four levels of interpretation, when speaking of the city of Jerusalem: "The four figures will be united, so that the same Jerusalem can take on four different meanings: in the historical sense, it will be the city of the Hebrews; in the allegorical sense, the Church of Christ; in the tropological sense, the human soul; in the anagogical sense, the celestial city, the mother of all of us." The Greek Fathers, on the other hand, presented a less precise distinction. Origen generally applies three levels of meaning in his commentaries on Scripture: literal, moral, and mystical, which correspond to the three constituent elements of the human being: body, soul, and spirit.[50] His successors generally reduce the different ways of reading to two major ones: the literal meaning and the symbolic meaning, which is the spiritual meaning (the literal meaning may or may not have a spiritual meaning). Nevertheless, the symbolic meaning is conceived in a broad sense which includes the allegorical, typological, tropological (or moral), and anagogic meanings.

While meanings other than the literal one were abandoned in Protestantism almost from its origin, and gradually by Roman Catholicism, from the Renaissance onwards, the Orthodox Church—without neglecting the literal meaning—gives them an essential place. This is why biblical studies in Orthodoxy needs to train students in perceiving these meanings, which reflect to the primary purpose of the Scriptures both in the ecclesial context and in that of the personal spirituality of the faithful.

Hermeneutics (the methodology of the interpretation of symbols) is a rather complex "science," which requires a very thorough apprenticeship, and needs to occupy a large part of the time devoted to biblical studies. This learning must go hand in hand with the study of the Fathers whose works are models of accomplished exegesis, and also with the study of the liturgical use of the texts, which contributes to drawing out their meaning. This shows once again that, contrary to the tendency toward the fragmentation of specialized studies, the different branches of theology need to be interconnected in accordance with the specific requirements of each of them.

Chapter V

Patrology

1. The Essential Place of Patrology in the Teaching of Orthodox Theology

Patrology or patristics is the subject devoted to the study of the Fathers of the Church.

This subject is only indirectly present in Protestant theology faculties. Protestantism attaches little importance to the Fathers of the Church and deals with them only incidentally, within the framework of the historical study of the first centuries of the Church. It has had a negative prejudice toward them ever since a current of Protestant thought in the nineteenth century (represented mainly by A. Harnack and his disciples), became practically official in Protestantism and has therefore been relayed into the twentieth century and up to the present day. This Protestant thought considered that the Fathers had led Christianity away from its primitive form, which had to be found by disregarding their thinking, to the extent that a Lutheran pastor and professor in a theology faculty said to me one day: "For us, between Luther and the Scriptures there is nothing."

Roman Catholicism grants the Fathers a greater place. Many Catholic scholars, since the twenties of the last century, have greatly contributed to the publication of critical editions of the writings of the Greek and Latin Fathers, and have devoted numerous studies to them. Many translations of the works of the Fathers had been made over the previous three centuries, fueling both the teaching of Catholic establishments and a significant amount of scholarly work. Certain differences exist, however, between Orthodoxy and Roman Catholicism as to the temporal extent of the patristic era and as to how to situate the works of the Fathers and their authority in the theological sphere. These we discuss in the study below. Within Orthodox theology, the Fathers have always had great importance, and patrology has always occupied a prominent place in theological teaching.

Today, however, throughout the Orthodox world, patristic studies are threatened by several factors, linked in particular to the deleterious influence of Western, Roman Catholic, and Protestant ideas and practices:

(1) There is a tendency to privilege minor authors, sometimes heretics (with a particular interest in the Syriac, Nestorian, or Monophysite sphere), to the detriment of major and Orthodox authors. In the same way as in the study of Scriptures, there is a tendency to favor apocryphal texts over canonical texts, or at least to study them on an equal footing, or to integrate them into studies on the same basis as canonical texts.
(2) The Fathers are often conceived and studied as philosophers, with the difference between the patristic mode of thought and the philosophical mode of thought no longer correctly perceived.
(3) As a result, modern patristic studies tend to neglect patristic filiations (the fact that the Fathers are inspired by the Fathers who preceded them), and to privilege philosophical filiations (Aristotelian, Platonic, and especially Neoplatonic). In this way sight is lost of the essential Orthodox notions of *Tradition* (in continuity of thought and in absolute fidelity to the kerygma) and of *catholicity* (the thought *according to the whole* [*kath'olon*] of the Church).
(4) In accordance with the Protestant methodology which also imposed itself on Roman Catholicism and which is closely linked with modern structuralist linguistics[51] (according to which in a structure it is the difference of each element from the others which gives it its

meaning), we study the differences between the Fathers rather than their common points or convergences. In this way one loses the essential Orthodox notion of *Patrum consensus*, which in the very name of these differences we tend to deny, as well as the criterion of truth laid down by St Vincent of Lérins: "what has always been believed, everywhere and by everyone." The result is a compartmentalization and then a complete fragmentation of patristic thought and patristic studies themselves, and a consequent loss of the sense of the unity of patristic thought, of its overall meaning and of its general direction.

(5) In line with the modern Roman Catholic approach inherited from the Protestant mentality, the Fathers are no longer perceived as living authors, our contemporaries in the communion of saints (as is well represented by the presence of their frescoes in our churches, where they stand shoulder-to-shoulder with the faithful), but are considered as outdated, as authors of a past era, in the same way as the writers of Antiquity or the Middle Ages. They are therefore studied at a critical distance, in their historical contexts, are viewed as outdated, and we no longer perceive the universal and timeless dimension of their teaching and therefore their interest and relevance for current theological thought and spiritual life. As a result, there is a tendency to reduce the place of patristic studies in the framework of theology, and to make it a sector of literary studies or historical studies.

I would like to recall here what, in an authentically Orthodox conception, should be the place of patrology within the framework of theological studies.

As a preliminary, it is necessary to recall first three principles that I presented in the first chapter concerning the Orthodox way of understanding theology.

(1) Orthodox theology is not an abstract, gratuitous speculation that permits innovation. Any theologian who theologizes within the Church places himself in the continuity of his Orthodox predecessors, and not in rupture with them.

(2) Orthodox theology may licitly have varying conceptual and verbal expressions, but it invariably expresses the same faith.
(3) Orthodox theology is part of Tradition.

For the Orthodox Church, Tradition has a triple basis: scriptural, conciliar, and patristic.

These three foundations are associated and interact in ecclesial life. The Fathers are for this reason "omnipresent" so to speak: the Councils express the consensus of the Fathers they have gathered; the Fathers are inspired, in their writings, by Scripture and previous Councils; Scripture in the Orthodox Church must be read in accordance with the faith as defined by the Councils and the understanding given to it by the Fathers.

Just as it is not possible to become part of the Orthodox Tradition while excluding Sacred Scripture and the holy Councils which have specified the correct faith (*orthè doxa*) by their definitions (*horoi*) and the right way of life (*ethos*) through their holy canons, it is not possible to be part of and express Tradition while excluding the Fathers.

Unlike the Roman Catholic Church, which today often considers the ancient Fathers as outdated ecclesiastical writers, and unlike Protestantism, which ignores the Church Fathers, skipping sixteen centuries from Scripture to Luther or Calvin, the Orthodox Church sets great store by the unbroken chain of the Fathers. From the Apostles to our present day, the Fathers have handed down among themselves and to us the faith bequeathed by Christ to His disciples. I say right up to the present day, because unlike the classical Roman Catholic conception, which considers the patristic period in the East to end with St John Damascene (eighth century) and in the West with Isidore of Seville (seventh century), the Orthodox Church considers that later centuries continued to produce Fathers and that the patristic era has no time limit.

2. The Importance of Knowledge of the Fathers for Theological Knowledge and Understanding

One of the reasons for the need to know the works of the Fathers well is their historical importance in the formation and development of Orthodox theology. It is through the struggle waged by St Athanasius of Alexandria and the Cappadocians Fathers against the Arians and the Pneumatomachi that the whole doctrine of the Trinity was precisely defined; it is thanks to the struggles of St Cyril of Alexandria against the Nestorians, of the Fathers of Chalcedon against the Monophysites, and of St Maximus the Confessor against the monoenergists and the monothelists, that Orthodox Christology was defined. Without an accurate study of these Fathers, it is virtually impossible to fully understand Orthodox theology concerning the Holy Trinity, the Holy Spirit, and Christ.

3. The Need for Reference to the Fathers in the Practice of Theology

It is necessary to refer to the Fathers not only for the knowledge and understanding of theology, but also for practicing it.

It is customary, in the practice of Orthodox theology, to refer to Scripture, liturgical texts, Councils, and the Fathers, because, as we have said, Orthodox theology is always integrated into Tradition and Tradition integrates all these. By referring to the Fathers and quoting them, the theologian shows that he is not expressing himself as an isolated individual. He is not taking his own self, his own conscience, his own thinking as his starting point, center, and reference. He does not consider himself an authority, but that his thought is integrated into a whole which is larger than himself and from which he draws his inspiration and finds the justification, value, and authority of what he affirms. Orthodox theological thought is not individualistic thought or even individual thought, but communal, Catholic thought (from *kath'olon*: according to the whole) where each member, not only now but throughout history, is—in the Body of Christ which constitutes the Church—in solidarity with the other members and derives from them his activity, his function, his legitimacy, and his authority. The Fathers are for the theologian all at once norms, guides, beacons, and supports. The theologian, by quoting the Fathers and deferring to them, testifies to his humility, to his submission to the teaching of the Church.

In this very process, the Fathers are models: all refer to their predecessors, and quote them, even if they do not always use explicit references, and even if they do not use quotation marks as we do today. The greatest among the Fathers defer to the other Fathers who preceded them by affirming that they owe everything to them and have thought nothing of their own. In this way St Maximus the Confessor, considered today as an original and particularly creative thinker, multiplies his expressions of fidelity to the teaching of the Fathers,[52] claiming to "follow the Holy Fathers in everything."[53] He testifies to his concern "to be entirely in the piety of and not to deviate from the teaching of the Fathers."[54] He affirms: "I think, I believe and I state the teaching of the Fathers as I received it from them."[55] Elsewhere he notes: "This is the faith which I have learned and which I continue to learn from our holy and blessed Fathers."[56] The expressions "according to the Fathers,"[57] "as the Fathers said,"[58] "as defined by the Fathers,"[59] "according to the teaching of the Fathers,"[60] "in accordance with the teaching of the well-tested Fathers,"[61] "with the Fathers,"[62] or "as transmitted to us by the teaching of the Fathers"[63] appear regularly under his pen. At the beginning of Letter 15, he states: "I will say nothing that comes from me, I will only express what the Fathers say, without changing anything."[64] St John Damascene, in the same way, writes at the beginning of his *Exact Exposition of the Orthodox Faith*: "All that has been passed on to us by the Law and the Prophets, as well as by the Apostles and the Evangelists, we receive it, we know it and we esteem it more than anything, and we desire nothing else. We will be fully satisfied with it and we will adhere to it, 'without removing the ancient landmark which the fathers have set' (Proverbs 22:28) or degrading the divine Tradition."[65]

4. On the Proper Use of the Fathers in the Practice of Theology

However, it is not enough to refer to the Fathers and to quote them—just as it is not enough to refer to Sacred Scripture and to quote it—to do good theology. There can be a good use and a bad use of the Fathers.

(a.) The bad use of the Fathers consists in the theologian placing them at the service of his own thought. It is indeed possible to develop a false concept and find quotations from the Fathers, taken out of context, to justify it. This can be seen in all heretics, but also in representatives of modern "Russian religious philosophy" such as Sergei Bulgakov or Paul Evdokimov.[66]

(b.) The proper use of the Fathers in theology presupposes that we first disregard our own thoughts and that, faced with a given problem or question, we first ask ourselves: "What do the Fathers think here?" On any subject he studies, the theologian should first collect all the texts of the Fathers which deal with it. He should then see what, despite the legitimate difference of patristic approaches (often linked to the difference in contexts), they have in common and draw direct inspiration from it for the treatment of his subject.

The theologian must always strive to think according to the Fathers, with the Fathers, like the Fathers. And for this he must be humble, set aside his individual opinion, and become impregnated, like a sponge one might say, with what the Fathers have said.

His personal intervention is then possible and legitimate in order to produce a synthesis. It is also possible in order to provide answers to questions which the Fathers did not answer because they did not arise in their time (for example, certain current questions of bioethics linked to the development of modern technologies), or because new errors of interpretation of dogma have appeared (there will indeed always be new heresies until the end of the world). But in this case, the theologian must always base himself on the principles laid down by the Fathers (e.g., for bioethics, on the anthropology that they elaborated, or for new heresies, on the dogmatic bases that they have already laid).

(c.) There is a difference in methodology between the Orthodox approach and the Roman Catholic and Protestant approach to the Fathers. As we have already noted, the Western university method is more sensitive to the differences between the Fathers than to what they have in common. On each point studied it is a question of showing how the thought of the particular Father one is studying differs from that of another Father. This method corresponds to the conception of the modern structuralist current according to which, within a structure, each element takes on its meaning and its value through its difference from the others. The Orthodox methodology derives from a different form of structuralism, which could be called "positive structuralism" or "unitive structuralism." It aims to bring out the common structure underlying the thought of the Fathers, which essentially unites the reflections of the Fathers beyond their differences. This common element corresponds to Tradition, of which we spoke previously, or to what is called the *Patrum consensus*, or again to the catholicity of the Church, that is what she conceives in her totality, her integrality, her universality.

5. Thinking in the Spirit of the Fathers

In cases where the theologian must express himself on subjects that the Fathers did not have the opportunity to address, he must think "like the Fathers," that is in the spirit of the Fathers.

a. To think in the spirit of the Fathers supposes first of all that he has become impregnated with this spirit by a long association with them, by an abundant reading of their works.

However, three points need to be clarified:

(1) It is important that theologians (and therefore first of all the students of theology and their professors) be trained by reading the classical Fathers, the great Fathers of the Church, and of course the Orthodox Fathers, and not the marginal Fathers or heterodox writers in whom many young theologians today are primarily interested, either because they are influenced by Roman Catholicism and especially Protestantism (which for two centuries has, in exegesis and patristic studies, systematically cultivated what is apocryphal or marginal), or because they seek a career in research and therefore opt by preference for original and little-discussed subjects.

(2) Training in the thought of the Fathers of the Church requires many years of intense and assiduous work. But today many students or young teachers write books or articles very soon after acquainting themselves with the authors they are talking about, and therefore produce mediocre work. A good understanding of Orthodox triadology and Christology requires several decades of study of the works of the Fathers who contributed to the elaboration of the dogma. Father Jean Meyendorff, an undisputed expert in patristic studies, once quipped that "one cannot understand anything about Christology before the age of 50."
(3) The third point to clarify is that there are several ways of reading the Fathers. There is an exterior, formal, and purely intellectual way of approaching them, as though they were philosophers or ancient writers. This way must be excluded for the Orthodox theologian. The Fathers must be approached with respect, as fathers in the first sense of the word and teachers (St Maximus the Confessor, in his works, constantly calls St Gregory the Theologian, from whom he draws much inspiration, "*o didaskalos*," the master). But above all they must be approached spiritually, with love and reverence. My spiritual father, the staretz Sergei (Chevitch), when I began to study the Fathers, advised me to read them in the same way as Sacred Scripture, not with the reason, but with the mind united with the heart, in prayer. This is how a true communion of spirit can be established with the Fathers, within the environment which is fundamentally theirs and which nourished their thought: that of spiritual and ecclesial life and experience.

b. A patristic way of thinking is acquired on the one hand by a certain intellectual imitation exercised in a certain inner spiritual atmosphere, but on the other hand and above all by thinking from the same spiritual dispositions as the Fathers, by having the same inner experience as them, and therefore also the same ecclesial and ascetic way of life as them. The theologian can only receive the discernment and inspiration he needs, which are a grace of the Holy Spirit, if he practices the divine commandments, purifies himself of the passions, strives to live according to the virtues, participates in liturgical life, is nourished by the Holy Mysteries in the ecclesial life, shows himself humble in relation to the Truth and to the Tradition of the Church which transmits it, and accomplishes his task out of love of God and neighbor.

6. The Continuing Relevance of the Fathers Today

The lessening of the space accorded to patrology in Orthodox theological educational establishments is largely the result of the influence of modernism which tends to give priority to modern authors and considers—as do Catholic and Protestant theological teaching establishments—that the Fathers are authors of a past era who must be studied as such, that they are outdated and cannot help us understand the problems that arise in the contemporary world. It is very characteristic in this respect that, at the Strasbourg Faculty of Protestant Theology, the Fathers are studied in the context of a subject entitled "History of Ancient Christianity," and that at the Faculty of Catholic Theology in the same city they are studied as part of a subject entitled "Ancient Christian Literature." In both cases, their "ancientness"—and therefore their outdatedness and irrelevance for current theology—is affirmed. In the first case, it is considered that they can only be the subject of a historical approach; in the second case, they are presented as literary authors, thus implicitly asserting that they have no more importance or authority than other literary authors of the same period. It is typical that in both faculties, the professors who teach these two subjects do not have specific training in the patrological field. For many generations at the Faculty of Protestant Theology, teachers have been specialists (more precisely editors) of apocryphal Scriptures, while at the Faculty of Catholic Theology they have a training in "Classics," essentially linguistic in nature (ancient Greek and Latin).

Compared with these approaches which consist of entrusting the teaching of patristic subjects to historians and above all to linguists and literature specialists, it is important that the Orthodox theological academies and seminaries entrust the teaching of patrology to authentic patrologists whose training is above all theological, even if knowledge of ancient languages is an essential prerequisite, as is a knowledge of the main modern scientific languages—French, German, English, Italian—in order to have access to secondary studies.

But what must above all be made clear here is that the Orthodox understanding of the place of the Fathers differs radically from the Roman Catholic conception, and even more so from the Protestant one. According to the Orthodox conception, the Fathers are neither ancient authors (i.e., they are not outdated or obsolete), nor authors just like any others (such as the philosophers or profane writers of antiquity).

On the one hand, they are integrated into current theological thought as authors who are relevant today. This is explained by what we have said about Tradition, which implies a continuity which transcends time, and which encompasses all the members of the body of Christ in the catholicity of the Church, which is not only a spatial universality but also a temporal universality. We can say that, in the realm of theology today, the Fathers, through their writings, profile themselves as our contemporaries in the same way as, in the space of the church, through the frescoes representing them, they become the contemporaries of the faithful who participate in the liturgy. The "communion of saints" includes also the field of theology.

On the other hand, unlike philosophers and writers, they enjoy a special authority in the Orthodox Church. They are literally *fathers* of the Church; it is they who, following the Apostles and as their successors, expressed and clarified the faith of the Church, explained the Orthodox meaning of the Scriptures, formulated the dogmas. Their thought and their writings definitely possess normative value. Within the Orthodox Church, their authority cannot be relativized either in relation to that of other authors, nor by the theologian who refers to them. Their works cannot be subjected to critical judgment in the same way as are ordinary philosophical or literary works. They should be treated with respect and, dare we say it—at the risk of shocking some secularized Orthodox readers—with piety.[67]

To the question often asked by people outside the Orthodox Church (Roman Catholics and Protestants), but also increasingly by young Orthodox theologians influenced by Western modernism: "Are not these ancient authors, the Fathers now outdated?" I would also like to respond from my personal experience: since I began to study the Fathers almost fifty years ago, I have always found that their thought and the way they express it remain surprisingly alive, and I would even say contemporary. That is what attracted me to reading them originally, and that is why I still find value in frequenting their works today.

I observe that my experience is shared by many people: one does not have the impression, in reading the Fathers (directly, and not through commentaries), of being in the presence of men who are far distant from us in space and time, even if some of them lived in distant times and in geographical and sociocultural contexts very different from our own. What they say speaks to us immediately and touches us directly.

There are several reasons for this: first the fact that they deeply live what they say, that it is not an abstract, artificial construction of their reason but an expression of their inner personal experience, where the intelligence finds itself intimately united with the heart; second, the fact that their teachings are constantly nourished by Scripture, which is also one of the main sources of our own Christian life; third, the fact that they live Christianity in a fundamental, in its most essential way, which has enabled their words and their writings to survive the centuries and nourish us even today; fourth, the fact that the thought of the Fathers (except in a few cases where the theology, because of the nature of the controversy, takes on a very technical aspect) is a concrete, existential thought; fifth, finally, the fact that their experience is universal in time and space, because this experience is that of life in Christ, who is, as St Paul says, "the same yesterday, today and forever" (Hebrews 13:8).

7. Studying the Fathers in Their Works and Not in the Commentaries on Them

To perceive the living and contemporary character of the Fathers, but also to become impregnated with their spirit and assimilate it, it is essential to read them directly, in their own works, and not through those of their modern commentators.

Of course, knowledge of ancient or modern commentaries, of studies that have been undertaken of the writings of the Fathers, is not only useful, but necessary, for the reasons and within the limits that I will set out in the next section. But it must be acquired secondarily. The first step must be to read the original texts themselves, and in the spirit and manner that I have previously described. But nowadays, the study of the Fathers is first approached through historical or theological studies which interfere. Not only are the Fathers not known in their own spirit and style, but they are known in an abstract way, from a generally historical and philological vantage point (the historical-philological method having long since become normative in Western academic patristic studies), and through an interpretative filter, the veracity of which is not fully guaranteed by the (relative) scientific method used. The problem of the quality of the interpretation is due not only to the preconceptions of the commentator, but to the greater or lesser extent of his knowledge of the work of the author he is studying. Two factors intervene here to limit the quality of the interpretations.

The first is that the universally accepted criteria of university research (implied by the organization of studies from the master's degree onwards in establishments that adhere to the "Bologna

Process"[68]) require that the dissertations and theses which for the most part constitute the referenced patristic studies deal with an original subject, that is to say, which has not yet been treated. This results in the production of increasingly specialized works focusing on a particular aspect or part of an author's work. This leads to the situation where this work is often no longer known and understood in its entirety, thus preventing a correct understanding of each of its parts—just as if one studies an organ of a living being without knowing the totality of the organism, we cannot correctly know its nature and its functioning.

The second relates to the obligation—now universal—for students preparing doctoral theses to publish outlines of their work, partial studies in the form of articles. This being done before they have acquired a comprehensive knowledge and understanding of their subject (because it is only at the end of the research work that these can have a definitive and sure form), these outlines are often of poor quality, as those with a thorough knowledge of the authors studied can perceive.

It is therefore the direct reading of the work of a Father as a whole that best enables us to understand it not only in its entirety, but also in its particular elements and, it should be added, in its proper context. This last point is also important, because there is always the risk, in studying a work through its commentators, of reading and understanding it in an anachronistic or biased way. A work must first be understood on its own.

8. Methodology of Patristic Studies in the Field of Research

The foregoing considerations apply to the study of the Fathers and the teaching of their thought in the framework of theological studies, the purpose of which is to practice theology internally (within the Orthodox Church itself) or to give general education, in-depth or not, for students destined for ministry in the Church.

These methodological considerations need to be spelled out for students required to carry out research work which will be read beyond the limits of the Church (in particular by their publication in journals or in editorial collections of an international character), and even more so for students who intend to pursue research professionally.

Studies and commentaries on the works of the Fathers (generally referred to as "secondary literature") should be taken into account for two main reasons.

1. The first reason relates to the choice of a research subject. If one does research work according to current universally accepted academic criteria, this research has to cover an original subject, that is to say one which has not yet been dealt with. It is necessary to establish a *status quæstionis* to learn which areas need to be developed for a given topic. To do this, one needs to carry out a bibliographical search extending to all the secondary literature. The prospective researcher needs to have a good understanding of the subject concerned, having examined it thoroughly. For this reason it is essential to have a knowledge of the main scientific languages in use in patristics (French, German, English, Italian). A shortcoming of a certain number of studies carried out in the United States or in Russia is that they are based only on a knowledge of the English language in the first case, and of the Russian language in the second case. The outcome is a multitude of redundant studies, useless because they have already been done in another language, and which fail to meet the criterion of originality required by genuine international-level university research.

As far as the choice of subject is concerned, one of the faults already pointed out is that many young researchers tackle secondary subjects that are without interest for their own training, and of little interest for their potential readers in the Orthodox sphere. Often these subjects take the place of fundamental subjects that researchers could have benefited from by having worked on more deeply and perfected their own training, and which would also have been much more useful for their potential readers. Often, the subjects chosen present the risk of alienating from Orthodoxy those who work on them and those who will learn the results of their study. For example, in recent decades studies have multiplied which are devoted to heretical authors from the Syriac language sphere of Monophysitism and Nestorianism. Orthodox researchers who work in these fields are often led, because of Western influences linked to their training abroad or their reading of secondary Catholic, Anglican, Protestant, or agnostic literature, to relativize the heterodoxy of authors and of doctrines even those considered heretical by the Orthodox Tradition.[69] Another fault is, under the same influences, to relativize the Orthodoxy of certain Orthodox authors.[70]

A good subject, in the framework of Orthodox patristic studies, is one which permits the student to deepen his or her knowledge of the thought of an author on a fundamental theme. In this way we tap into the catechetical purpose of theology. A good subject is also one that allows for the rectification of previous misinterpretations of an author's thinking. Here we link in with the apologetic purpose of theology. An excellent subject is one that offers the possibility of achieving both these goals.

2. We encounter here the second reason why a knowledge of secondary literature is useful and even necessary: it gives access to the multitude of interpretations of a Father's thought on a given theme. Some topics lend themselves easily to agreement, but others are the subject of significant divergence and even controversy. We expect a study to take account of all the interpretations and end up by adopting a position that conforms as closely as possible to the thought of the author studied.

We said earlier that an author must be understood on his own terms, in his own context. When it comes to the study of the Fathers of the Church, it happens that honest studies, exempt from *a prioris* and prejudices, attain a remarkable level of objectivity, whatever the researcher's denominational affiliation. Such qualities are found in studies conducted by Protestant[71] or Catholic[72] scholars who do not start out with ready-made interpretative systems, or even with an ideology which constitutes an interpretive grid to which the texts are systematically subjected, as is the case with a large number of Catholic researchers who strongly adhere to the doctrine of Thomism,[73] or seek, on dogmatic questions, to align themselves with the magisterium and to confirm the various innovations of Roman Catholicism since the ninth century (filioque, purgatory, immaculate conception, primacy of power and infallibility of the pope, doctrine of created grace, etc.).

The adherence of Orthodox researchers to the Orthodox Tradition offers them serious assets for a good understanding of the patristic texts for the reasons that we have previously given: the Fathers are theologically our contemporaries. Traditional Orthodox theology is a living and faithful continuation of the thought of the Fathers, which is not the case either with Catholic theology (which has undergone a certain number of innovations compared to it), or with Protestant theology which explicitly affirms a break with it (to the point of accusing the Fathers of infidelity to original Christianity).

However, Orthodox researchers are not immune to excesses in their interpretations, for example by emphasizing a particular Father for the understanding of certain others, giving rise to conflicts with Catholic researchers,[74] but also sometimes to tensions within Orthodoxy itself.[75] Although, according to the Orthodox conception, the Fathers are situated in the same general line and all bear witness to the Catholic faith of the Church, it is important, from a methodological point of view, to respect the identity of each by studying his thought in his own context[76] while taking into account his relationships with others in his ancestry and filiation or influences.

The historical-philological method which has become normative in the framework of international university studies can be used with profit, but must be modulated in such a way as to avoid certain excesses to which it has given rise, and to preserve the Orthodox identity which we have evoked in the previous sections.

It has become fashionable in recent years to emphasize philosophical ancestry—Stoic, Aristotelian, Platonic, and Neoplatonic—in the study of the thought of the Fathers, with, in recent years, a strong tendency to privilege the latter and to multiply studies linking the Fathers with Neoplatonist thinkers. This trend emerged in the nineteenth century in Protestant circles (A. Harnack and his followers believed that the Greek Fathers were massively influenced by Platonism and thereby seriously adulterated the original message of Christianity). This viewpoint was relayed by Catholic patrologists,[77] though without sharing the radicalism of Protestant positions, and sometimes bringing important nuances to the nature of the influences undergone,[78] but not without at times an underlying desire to devalue certain features of the thought of the Greek Fathers in comparison with that of the Latin Fathers,[79] or in relation to the concurrent influence of Aristotelianism in medieval authors, especially Thomas Aquinas and his posterity. This tendency has been accentuated in recent years in Catholic circles (which have especially favored Neoplatonism, or Aristotelianism revisited by the Neoplatonists), and has been passed on by imitation to a certain number of Orthodox patrologists.

In most of these studies, which follow a methodology adapted to secular literature, we encounter a misunderstanding of the nature of patristic thought.

In a certain number of cases, false affiliations have been established due to commentators' insufficient knowledge of the patristic literature itself: certain ideas or expressions are attributed to Neoplatonic sources in place of the patristic sources that these commentators have failed to recognize.[80]

Above all, there is a misunderstanding of the process of transformation to which the Fathers subjected the concepts that they borrowed from philosophies foreign to Christianity. It is true that the notions of "essence," "nature," "hypostasis," and "person," for example, do not appear in the Scriptures and that the Fathers borrowed them from Greek philosophy when, faced with heresies, they needed to specify Orthodox Trinitarian theology and Christology. But they assimilated these notions, Christianized them, and changed their nature and meaning, so that if formally they resemble or are identical to notions of Greek philosophy, they no longer have, in substance, the same relation to them. And this can be applied to many other notions such as that of "Logos" (used to designate the Son of God), or that of *"logos"* (plural *logoi*), which is frequently used by St Maximus the Confessor, but the philosophical source of which it is impossible to determine, as St Maximus integrated it into his system of thought and made it a concept of his own. A better-known example is that of the word *prosopon* which in Greek designates the theater mask, and which the Greek Fathers chose to designate both divine and human persons, thus giving it a radically different meaning. Father Georges Florovsky spoke a lot about this subject, on the one hand because he advocated a "re-Hellenization" of theology and a preservation of the Greek vocabulary, and on the other hand because, correlatively, he wanted to emphasize that the Hellenism of the Greek Fathers (which according to him the first Latin Fathers also shared) had nothing to do (except in a purely formal and external way) with the Hellenism of the Greek philosophy with which the school of Harnack and his disciples sought to identify it.[81]

These considerations give us the opportunity to insist once again on the necessity, in the framework of patristic studies, of correctly establishing filiations, ancestry, and descent. Systematically seeking and prioritizing philosophical ancestry, as is often done today, not only fails to respect the reality of the texts but also fails to respect the spirit of the Fathers who in most cases distanced themselves from the philosophers, and who in integrating philosophy gave it a particular meaning: that of the specifically Christian way of life. On the other hand, they were almost always inspired by their predecessors, although they only rarely give their names and quote them without quotation marks, as was the wont in their time.[82]

Another defect of the historical-philological method in force in Western teaching and research institutions (whether Catholic, Protestant, Anglican, or agnostic) that we have already pointed to is its bias toward emphasizing the differences and oppositions between authors, following the principles of modern structuralism, according to which it is these that give meaning. As we have already noted, this gives rise to a total fragmentation of patristic thought and of patristic studies themselves, and thus to a loss of any sense of the unity of patristic thought, of its overall meaning and its general direction. Orthodox research work cannot be satisfied with this methodology because it does not correspond to the conception that Orthodoxy has of the positive and unitive relations that the Fathers have between themselves within the Church conceived in its catholicity. The *Consensus patrum* can no doubt be found wanting on secondary points of doctrine where there is room for personal opinions or what in the twentieth century have been called *theologoumena*, but this consensus is a reality that can be seen within the patristic works themselves, a consensus that certain Fathers like St Maximus the Confessor or St John Damascene explicitly affirmed, and that St Vincent of Lérins briefly theorized. Orthodox methodology must therefore assert its specificity in this area. Without refusing to note the differences and without failing to mention them, it must establish an inverse priority, favoring what brings the Fathers together more than what distinguishes them, and shedding light, according to the principles of what one might call a "positive" or "unitive" structuralism, on the common underlying structure of their conceptions and formulations. This approach does not deviate from the scientific criteria currently required in the field of specialized patristic studies; it is simply an alternative approach to the currently dominant approach. It requires just as much rigor, demonstrative capacity, and precision as the latter, and in truth corresponds more adequately to its object (in other words allows a more objective study) insofar as, as can be seen in their works, the Fathers constantly take care to cite the Fathers who preceded them to show that they are in the same line as them, and that they are in agreement with them as to the substance, as some of them moreover explicitly assert.[83]

Chapter VI

Church History

Church history obviously plays an extremely important role in theological education. Inevitably, like other theological subjects, Church history interrelates with other disciplines such as dogmatic theology, patrology, liturgical theology, exegesis, hagiology, or iconology.

Like all forms of history, Church history is a presentation of a succession of events, and more broadly of the facts that have marked the Church over time, from its origins to the present day, and that have contributed to making it what it is today, not in its essence, already defined by the teaching of Christ and the apostles, but in the forms of expression of its faith, in its rites and its institutions.

The goal of Church history is the same as that of the history of societies and civilizations: having the past as its object, history seeks not only to acquaint us with the past in itself, but also to help us better understand the present, insofar as the present is to a large extent the continuation and the consequence of the past. It therefore answers the questions that the man of today asks about the past. For this it depends to a large extent on the way the man of today looks on the past.

History is dependent on our viewpoint, which is the first reason why we cannot speak of absolute objectivity in history. But nor is history subjective and random; it is based on facts, reported by documents, the authenticity and veracity of which are in principle verified. The contribution of modern historical science to Church history needs to be stressed here, in particular the critical method which operates at two levels: that of the authenticity of documents (dating, author, etc.) which is established by external criticism, and that of the veracity of their content (reliability of testimonies, extent and limits of the information transmitted, etc.) which is established by internal criticism. Both levels of the critical method involve the comparison of varied sources and their respective evaluation.

But at the same time, contrary to a widespread prejudice, the facts do not speak for themselves. This is why the definition we gave at the beginning of this chapter of history as being "a presentation of the succession of events, and more broadly of the facts which have marked the Church over time" requires clarification. Simply listing the facts in their chronological order is not enough to constitute history. The facts must be placed in their context, their causes and their consequences known (and therefore linked together), evaluated as to their real importance (measured mainly by their effects, which presupposes a certain hindsight), understood as to their significance (meaning and orientation), and therefore also, with regard to these last two points, interpreted.

Very often the interpretation of the facts takes on a hypothetical character (this hypothetical character being even accentuated in the framework of a scientific methodology). In history, the plausibility of hypotheses is guaranteed by having a certain number of unverifiable documents, as is the case in the natural sciences where hypotheses are confronted with direct observations or verifications in the form of reproducible experiments, which is doubly impossible in history because the facts are past and are always unique.

These different parameters, although well-framed and protected from significant irregularities, nevertheless leave room for a variety of interpretations depending on certain *a prioris*, which can give the history of certain facts and certain periods in the past noticeably different shapes. This is the second reason why we cannot speak of absolute objectivity in history.

The history of the Church is inevitably oriented by the conception that we have of the Church, of its nature, of its structure, of the direction of its evolution, etc. This is most striking when history is understood in the light of a "philosophy of history" (as found in St Augustine's *The City of God*). In the history of the Church elaborated within the Roman Catholic Church, the central and dominant importance accorded to the pope during the second millennium has a considerable impact, as does the theory, widely accepted since the nineteenth century, of the development of dogma, as well as the spirit of the Counter-Reformation (under the impulse of the Council of Trent). Moreover, the appearance of new beliefs or new dogmas, such as the filioque, purgatory, the Immaculate Conception, the primacy of power, and the infallibility of the pope of Rome have led to a rereading of history to seek elements likely to justify these innovations (with a high rate of misinterpretations and falsifications). In the histories of the Church developed in Protestant denominations, the rejection of a certain number of Roman Catholic developments dating from the centuries preceding the Reformation and the desire for a return to the first sources of Christianity brought about, as we noted in the previous chapter, a devaluation of the contribution of the Greek Fathers, supposedly strongly influenced by a Hellenic heritage alien to primitive Christianity, and more generally an undervaluation of the period separating the first two centuries of Christianity from the Reformation.

To all this must be added an important consideration: for the Orthodox Church, the history of the Church represents something special in relation to the history of the civilizations or societies within which it has developed. The Church was founded by Christ (it began with the community of the Apostles), and spread throughout the world through the mission of the apostles, giving it not only a natural human dimension, but also a supernatural charismatic dimension. Subsequently, throughout its history, the Church was animated and oriented by the Holy Spirit, and constituted, in all the societies where it was established, a kind of parallel society (the ecclesial community, the Body of the Christ, an anticipation of the Kingdom of Heaven). It was certainly, outwardly and formally, an institution analogous to all social institutions, but it was also, inwardly, essentially and mystically, a divine institution obeying other laws than those of societies of "this world," and governed (managed, directed, and energized) by divine Providence.

For all these reasons, the history of the Church as elaborated in the Orthodox Church has different forms and content from the histories elaborated within the Roman Catholic Church and the Protestant denominations, especially in modern times when these have been strongly secularized. This can be seen very clearly, for example, by comparing histories of the Church developed by Roman Catholic historians and Protestant theologians (like A. von Harnack [see especially his classic works *Das Wesen des Christentums* and *Lehrbuch der Dogmengeschichte*] or members of his school) with those written by Orthodox historians, for example the seven-volume *Histoire de l'Église* by Father Vladimir Guettée, a Catholic convert to Orthodoxy. Fr Vladimir was well aware of the differences and would not have ventured on this enormous undertaking if similar works on the history of the church, produced in the framework of other Christian denominations, had seemed to him reliable from an Orthodox point of view, and if it had not seemed essential to him to resume such work despite the cost.

It follows from these considerations that the history of the Church in Orthodox theological teaching cannot simply reproduce the church histories developed in Roman Catholic or Protestant contexts, nor take them as standards and models.[84] However, certain relatively neutral works may provide useful information and a bases for reflection.

Certain scientific methods used by these histories are also useful (and even necessary) and can benefit historical research on the Orthodox Church and undertaken within its framework. These are in fact methods borrowed from profane or secular science and which focus primarily on the quality of the documents used, and not the very understanding of history and the interpretation of the facts, their relationships and their meaning, which cannot be dissociated from an awareness that the Orthodox Church has its own identity.

The very vast field, in space and time, of the history of the Church practically implies that its teaching be subdivided. If the history of the Church of the first eight centuries can constitute a unit, the formation with Charlemagne of an independent and increasingly divergent Western Church makes it necessary to constitute a section dedicated to the history of the Western Church, with this section again splitting into two subsections from the Reformation onwards, which can be grouped under the title of "History of Western confessions." But it is possible, for the period preceding the break, to establish three sections: history of the ancient Church; history of the Byzantine Church; history of the Latin Church. More recently the gradual granting of autocephaly to Eastern Churches with increasingly marked specificity and independence justifies the establishment of a section dedicated to the history of local Orthodox Churches.

It is also important to reserve a section for the history of the heterodox Eastern Churches—Nestorian and Monophysite—generally called non-Chalcedonian, in particular because of their interaction, for several centuries, with the local Orthodox Churches of the Middle East. This study is moreover useful in understanding their current status, which is not always clear in the consciousness of the clergy and of certain Orthodox theologians.

Chapter VII

Moral Theology and Bioethics

1. Moral Theology

"Moral theology" is almost always part of any course of theological studies.

First of all, we need to point to the problematic nature of this title.

Many Orthodox writers today insist that Orthodoxy is not about morality, and does not, strictly speaking, contain a moral system.

To a certain extent they are right in affirming this, even if religion in general and Christianity in particular are often viewed by the non-Christian public as moral systems. Morality is rather frowned upon in the contemporary world, and criticized for its formal character, at least when considered in itself and presenting itself, as is often the case, as a set of rules which define what is authorized and, in particular, prohibited. Already in the seventeenth century, Pascal criticized this formal morality which gives rise to what is called moralism, affirming: "True morality couldn't care less about morality." In the absence of interest in dogma and the liturgical life, but also and above all in the absence of spirituality (and of what we in Orthodoxy call the *ascetic life* in the broad sense), a large part of Protestantism found itself reduced to no more than a moral system, first of all individual then social, thereby contributing to its decadence in the Western world. Sociologists also consider that under the pontificate of John Paul II, the pope's moralizing speeches (in particular on contraception) gave

Catholicism an image that was harmful to it and contributed to its loss of audience in contemporary society.

Though Orthodoxy refuses to be assimilated to a moral system and even to see itself as implementing a moral code, this does not, however, mean that it is amoral. It obviously has a notion of good and evil, of their difference and their distinction (which is the basis of all morality). It also advocates a certain way of life, which tries to avoid evil and conform to good (St Maximus the Confessor considered that the duty of man, who has received "being," is to acquire "being-well," so as to receive in the Kingdom the grace of "always-well-being"). The word "moral" comes from the Latin mores, a word also found in English, which means "ways of living." But Orthodoxy, given the Hellenic roots of its vocabulary, prefers to use the Greek word ethos, which means "kind of life," thereby circumventing the word "morality" and its disadvantages we have already noted. Nor does it use the word "ethics" derived from ethos and widely used today in quite diverse secular fields, so as not to fall into the field of principles and rules, but to retain the idea that true morality is for Orthodoxy the Christian way of life, which does not consist in obedience to rules which authorize or prohibit, but in a certain state of mind that guides behavior, albeit with reference to certain standards, but which are not of a legal nature.

The Christian way of life is often designated by the word *asceticism* or *ascesis,* taken in its broad sense, where it designates life according to the virtues and the struggles against the passions on which this is predicated. If we want to keep the notions of good and evil, we can say that good consists in the adherence to the various virtues in behavior, acts, thoughts, dispositions, attitudes, and states, while evil consists in non-conformity to these, the passions being that which opposes the virtues, preventing their emergence, manifestation, and development. The virtues together constitute what St Maximus the Confessor calls "being-well" (εὖ εἶναι).

The virtues have their primary foundation in Christ, whom St Maximus the Confessor designated as "the essence of the virtues." The ascetic life in its broad sense is therefore "life in Christ" (according to the expression used by Sts. Nicholas Cabasilas and John of Kronstadt to summarize their presentations of the spiritual life), the person of Christ, with His attitudes and His behavior as revealed to us by the Gospels being the reference and the supreme norm of the Christian ethos. This is known to us also through the lives of the saints, who are those Christians who have perfectly realized the likeness of Christ in this world.

We therefore see that what corresponds to "morality" is what in Orthodoxy is known as "asceticism." In some Orthodox theological academies, they do teach not "moral theology," but instead "ascetic theology," which undoubtedly corresponds better to the spirit of Orthodoxy.

The reference to virtues and passions may seem rather vague to people (including Christians, and even Orthodox Christians) who are not familiar with these concepts. But it is possible to make an extended study of them that encompasses all the behaviors, inner and outer attitudes, or states of the human being. The ascetic literature on this subject is immense, and there are summaries available.[85]

Here again we see that the different theological subjects cannot be kept totally independent but need to meet and combine, like the different members of the same body which need each other to exercise their functions. In this case, ascetic theology must absolutely be combined with patrology, for it is in the writings of the Holy ascetic Fathers that the ascetic way of life which constitutes true Orthodox morality is exposed in detail. Ascetic theology must also encounter hagiology, for the *Lives* of the Fathers illustrate for us this way of life in an even more concrete form.

2. Bioethics

Bioethics has become in our day a necessary extension of moral theology. Advances in science and medical technology have given rise to new problems which affect large numbers of people in our societies, and on which the Church is obliged to take positions, both in terms of principles and on the level of pastoral care, to inform and train pastors and to guide the faithful. A first series of problems concerns the origin of life (abortion, contraception, assisted reproduction, surrogacy, etc.); a second series concerns the end of life (euthanasia, artificial prolongation of life, palliative care and treatment of suffering, treatment of the body after death, cremation, etc.); a third series concerns intermediate care (organ transplantation, *enhancement*,[86] transhumanism, etc.).

The knowledge, understanding, and treatment of these problems require medical knowledge, which teachers and their students need to acquire.

The solutions brought to them must be defined within the framework of Orthodox Christian anthropology and ethics. These have been elaborated over the centuries, in particular by the Fathers who developed a general reflection and teaching on the body in its relationship to the soul, the origin of life, the status of the embryo and the fetus, the meaning of illness and suffering, death and life after death, the value of the human person, or who had to deal more precisely with one or another of the topics covered, such as contraception, abortion, or euthanasia. But the novelty of certain problems posed by radically new practices (relating in particular to medically assisted procreation or transhumanism) requires that new solutions be defined. These must be in the spirit of the Fathers and in the continuity of the principles already established by them. Syntheses of this order have been elaborated by various Orthodox theologians.[87] Reference to secular ethics in these matters is of no use, because on the one hand the Ethics Committees established by certain States, which give opinions (most often in relation to legislation) are composed of members adhering to various religions and philosophies with varied and sometimes very vague, even confused anthropological and ethical standards,[88] and on the other hand the laws enacted by the States are most often in response to societal desires or movements of opinion expressed by pressure groups that are sometimes very minority or marginal but nevertheless influential.[89]

On a number of bioethics issues, the Orthodox Church finds itself in agreement with the positions expressed by the Catholic Church in numerous documents (in particular papal encyclicals), but not completely coinciding with them. For example, for the Catholic Church, respect for life is an absolute norm that dictates its position in several bioethics-related areas, while for the Orthodox Church the norm is rather respect for the person, life being only an abstraction when considered apart from the living person and where its preservation as an intangible rule applicable to all cases can sometimes go against the true interests (spiritually of course) of the person.[90] Generally speaking, the Roman Catholic approach remains marked by the legalism that characterizes the Latin tradition, while the Orthodox approach is more flexible, less concerned with the strict application of identical rules in each and every case, but rather for the good of each person in the particular situation in which they find themselves and in relation to their particular spiritual needs. Here we have a practice that corresponds to the well-known distinction in the canonical domain between *acribia* and *oeconomia*. It is obviously impossible (and it would be contradictory) to train future pastors *a priori* to face the indefinite multitude of possible singular situations, but it is possible to give them the indispensable ethical principles and to help them acquire the spirit in which concrete application of these should take place.

The dominant Protestant denominations (among the multitude of groups and sub-groups of Protestantism) can be divided into two broad categories: (1) those which are attached to the two main majority currents in Europe, Lutheranism and Calvinism, and which maintain university institutions (often recognized by the States where they are established); (2) those which are connected with the evangelical current, which has seen a strong expansion in our day.

As far as the first category is concerned, the moralism that we mentioned earlier, if strict at its origins, has developed an ever more individualist and liberal drift, tolerance being a favorite watchword in matters not only of opinion but of behavior. Linked, as Max Weber has shown, to the origins and development of liberal capitalism, this category follows its current ultra-liberal evolution with, as its correlates, abolition of boundaries, rejection of universal reference values, and absolute priority given to individual choice. Although differing opinions are present, it generally accepts modern societal currents, as well as all societal reforms—sexual relations outside marriage, contraception and abortion without reservation, euthanasia, same-sex marriage, medically assisted procreation for homosexuals and single women, etc.—and even contributes to the promotion of these.

The second category generally defends a strict morality and therefore opposes all these practices, but in a spirit close to ancient moralism and in the framework of a fundamentalist reading of the Bible.

The liberal Protestant current is far removed from Orthodox positions in spirit and content. The evangelical current is closer to the character of the content but remains far from it in its spirit. The two currents can therefore interest Orthodox reflection only as examples of paths that must (continue to) be avoided. They can help keep it on the "royal road" in a globalized world whose benchmarks are tending to fade more and more, in the same way that the white lines placed on each side of the road help a car, even equipped with good headlights, to stay in the middle of the road in foggy weather or in the dark of the night.

Chapter VIII

Hagiology

Hagiology is a subject unknown to Protestant theological faculties, for the reason that Protestantism, in its various forms, has no veneration of the saints. Protestants generally consider saints, like the Mother of God, as unnecessary mediations between man and God, and even as harmful because of a risk of idolatry (adoring the creature in place of the creator) and giving to them a part of the piety due to God.

Hagiology no longer has a place either in the Faculties of Catholic Theology and has also lost a lot of space in the scholarly studies carried out within Catholicism. This is explained by the secularization that followed on the Second Vatican Council and by the influence of the "theological" current of demythologization, which affected the field of dogma, but even more so that of hagiography, now reputed to belong to the world of legends. Angels, the devil, demons and miracles, omnipresent in hagiographical accounts, have become foreign to the faith of a majority not only of the faithful but also of clerics, in particular the most "learned" among them who make up the teaching body.

It must be said, however, that during the seventeenth, eighteenth, and nineteenth centuries, Catholicism attached great importance to hagiography. The translations of *Lives of the Saints* received considerable impetus from the end of the seventeenth century (we know the important contribution, magnificent in its style, of Arnauld d'Andilly to the translation of the *Lives* of the Fathers and Mothers of the desert), but it is in the nineteenth century that major collections of lives of saints from all over the Christian world were published, the best known of which is *Les Petits bollandistes. Vies des saints*, published in fifteen volumes by Mgr Guérin in Paris between 1865 and 1869.[91] The learned society of the Bollandists (consisting exclusively of Jesuits), which began to specialize in hagiography in the middle of the seventeenth century with the publication of the *Acta Sanctorum* (lives of the saints following the order of the calendar), gave an increasingly scientific turn to its work, as far as to make its publications (in particular in the review *Analecta Bollandiana* and the two collections *Subsidia Hagiographica* and *Tabularium Hagiographicum*) an absolute reference in the matter.

The Bollandists' scientific method was characterized from the outset by its critical approach which undermined a certain number of elements considered legendary in the *Lives of the Saints* in circulation until then. This aroused within Catholicism itself, at the end of the seventeenth century, a movement of protest from the Benedictines and then the Carmelites, who even obtained a condemnation of the *Acta Sanctorum* by the Spanish Inquisition, which however was not confirmed by the Holy Office.

These works are today unanimously received. They are based on the application of scientific methods used in the fields of history (external and internal criticism) and the editing of critical texts, which we have already mentioned.

Hagiology is not taught as a scholarly discipline in all Orthodox academies (or colleges), but it should be. The veneration of saints indeed occupies an important place in Orthodox liturgical life and spirituality, and the reading of the *Lives of the Saints* is very important for the spiritual life of each Orthodox faithful, for reasons that St Justin Popović (†1979) highlighted in the brilliant introduction and conclusion of one of his major works, the *Lives of the Saints* in twelve volumes.

It is important that priests have reliable texts for their sermons, and the faithful for their personal spiritual reading.

This is not the case *a priori* of all hagiographic texts: their pious character not only is no protection against inaccuracies but encourages their authors to exaggerate or even tell "pious lies," some of which are even commonplaces in hagiography. Such non-truths can be found even in the Vitae of great spiritual contemporaries, presented, for example, as refusing the maternal breast as infants on fast days and during Lent so as not to absorb a dairy product proscribed by the canons, or even—which is perfectly ridiculous—already sporting small beards. Such exaggerations are obviously counterproductive: they cast doubt on the other elements contained in the hagiographies concerned. In terms of the spiritual objectives of these texts, which by presenting their subject as being somehow holy from birth devalue any efforts the saint might have made during his life to receive the grace of holiness.

A good number of legends are mixed in with the *Lives of the Saints*. Some are repeated in several of them, constituting what are called "commonplaces" (*topoi* in technical language). Critical examination of the texts often reveals that passages have been copied outright from one *Life* to another, and borrowings from other *Lives* often serve the hagiographer to fill in the blanks, that is to make good the lack of information on a particular period or an episode of the life he is relating. It is commonplace for the saint's psychological and spiritual character to be invented, and for his virtues to be exaggerated compared to the source data.

Another common fault, especially in the Greek-speaking world, and even today when writing the *Lives* of great contemporary spiritual persons, is to multiply the flourishes and effects of style, and also to maintain an atmosphere of sentimentality and pietism.

Orthodox hagiography must be at once truthful and sober. And for this, it is undoubtedly valuable for it to have recourse at a primary level to Western scientific methods which allow one to match back with their sources texts which have been the subject of superfluous additions.

But critical editions are not enough, for sometimes the original sources themselves are inflationary or legendary in character. It even quite often happens that saints' *Lives* are written several centuries after their death, based on popular accounts transmitted from generation to generation, undergoing alterations and distortions (in the form of amplification or loss) in the process.

However, the oral sources—exclusive or partial—that we have are not necessarily dubious, because sometimes, for various reasons (e.g., persecutions and censorship), the oral transmission of the facts was preferable to their immediate transcription, and those undertaking the transmission did so in a scrupulous way. We can also observe that popular memory is able to retain facts faithfully for long periods of time.

It should also be noted that the Church has endorsed with its authority certain facts that are poorly established by the texts. Certain saints also at times receive supernatural revelations concerning certain episodes in the lives of saints of the past, and the truth of these revelations can sometimes be confirmed by facts, as, for example, in the rather frequent cases where unknown relics are discovered following these revelations, and where unknown saints are discovered in this way.

These different aspects need to be taken on board by Orthodox hagiography, because the Orthodox Church on the one hand recognizes a certain value in popular traditions, and on the other hand admits the possibility of particular supernatural revelations, considering that the Holy Spirit is at work in his saints and gives them by grace possibilities of knowledge which go beyond that of the senses and reason.

But in general, truth requires that we remain silent about what we do not know or discreet about what we know little about and that we avoid any temptation to fill in the "blanks" with imagination or by commonplaces, even for pious reasons. There exist in hagiography a multitude of saints of whom only the name has been kept, and, in the case of martyrs, only the form and place of their martyrdom; it is necessary to stick to these data, however disappointing their incomplete character.

However, hagiography cannot disregard the purpose of the *Lives of the Saints,* and therefore cannot be limited to simple historical facts, and even less to a criticism of sources as a purely scientific hagiography tends to do.[92]

The use of platitudes to supplement insufficient data and even the integration of legendary elements can themselves find justification in relation to the purpose of the lives of the saints within the framework of Orthodox spirituality, as the hieromonk Macarius of Simonos Petra, one of the best contemporary Orthodox hagiographers, explains: "the 'legendary' and rhetorical dimension of the *Lives of the Saints* is part of the 'hagiographic discourse' which has its specificity and its function in the life of the Church. It is a phenomenon in every way similar to iconography, which has its own 'discourse', its stylistic procedures which differentiate it from painting. It is a question of bringing the faithful into a transfigured world, thanks to conventional means, which constitute a sort of tacit code, which the Orthodox faithful have assimilated since childhood." We can add that we find a similar phenomenon in liturgical hymnology where the services devoted to saints evoke in part the facts of their lives, but also, and to a greater extent, their spiritual qualities and charisms, according to stylistic processes specific to these compositions, aimed at bringing the faithful into a process of liturgical prayer where praise and petition are combined.

It is normal that the virtues found in the lives of the saints, as far as we know them, be highlighted as much as possible, as theses virtues often shine through in their way of life or in the way they confront certain events (e.g., patience in trials, courage in martyrdom). A hagiography differs from a simple biography.[93] It is legitimate that these virtues, if they do not appear directly in historical data, be induced, a saint being by definition a Christian who has acquired a high degree of virtue, and even all the virtues since, according to the classical teaching of the Fathers, all the virtues are interlinked. Here the comparison with iconography is relevant: for in the icons, the virtues of the saints are revealed, and the Orthodox faithful contemplating them perceive the virtues intuitively and appropriate them in part through the contemplation.

It is also legitimate that, as facts observed by witnesses, the miracles performed should not be concealed because of their non-rational nature, but should on the contrary be brought to light and even valued as evidence of a supernatural reality inherent in holiness and its radiance. Under the influence of the demythologization promoted by a number of theologians as part of the global movement of secularization, there is a suspicion hanging over the Catholic world and even more in the Protestant world with respect to miracles. This suspicion does not exist in the Orthodox world. The reality of miracles continues to be experienced in Orthodoxy daily, especially with the relics and icons of saints.

A work coming close to scientific methodology (which was only well established from the nineteenth century onwards) was accomplished by certain orthodox hagiographers such as St Nicodemus the Hagiorite in the Greek-speaking world or St Dimitri of Rostov in the Slavic world, who produced syntheses by comparing sources. A further step toward being truthful and sober while respecting the spiritual purpose of Orthodox hagiography has been taken by contemporary Orthodox hagiographers such as Archimandrite (now Saint) Justin Popović in his *Lives of the Saints*, or more recently by Hieromonk Macarius of Simonos Petra in his *Synaxarion*, which is today a reference in the Orthodox world (although presenting the *Lives of the Saints* only in summary form to encourage the daily reading of the faithful and reading in monastery refectories). One can see in his synthetic notes and their annotations that Hieromonk Macarius takes into account all the preceding hagiographic literature, including the contradictory, and critically assesses it. He succeeds in finding a balance between the requirements we have mentioned, at least in the tension.

Chapter IX

Iconology

Iconology is an Orthodox specialty, as are icons themselves. It is a subject rarely taught in seminaries and theological academies, because it is deemed to belong in a training cycle centered on iconography, provided parallel to theological training.

It is important, however, that iconology be studied as part of theological training, given (1) its strong dogmatic implications, as manifested during the two periods of iconoclasm, in the treatises of several Church Fathers who took part in the fight against the iconoclasts, and in the discussions and the Definition of the Seventh Ecumenical Council (Nicaea II); (2) the prominent place of the icon in the Orthodox worship—corporately and privately—and on various levels, ecclesial, private, catechetical, and its overall impact on the spiritual life of the faithful.

But in this field too, certain methodological principles must be established, in order to make this study fruitful and to preserve Orthodox identity by avoiding certain risks of deviations.

First of all, it is important not to confuse iconology with art history. This is unfortunately what has been done and continues to be done in the West where the meaning of the icon is not perceived, owing to the failure to place it in its ecclesial context and to understand its essentially spiritual purpose. In the West iconography can be viewed as one art form among others.

In this approach, the focus is above all on distinguishing and dating schools of iconography, identifying and assessing iconographers (perceived as artists, more or less original, more or less talented), whereas from the point of view of what the icon essentially is in the Church and for the Orthodox faithful, these points are quite secondary and even totally negligible. This approach was unfortunately also that of the icon specialists of the Soviet era, who either lacked the spiritual bases, or the social possibility (i.e., owing to the censorship exercised by the communist state) to present the icon differently. This has also played a positive role since many icons, being treated as works of art, were preserved from destruction in the same way as works of art in general. The Soviet era is over, but this method of approaching the icon can still be found in the countries of the former Soviet Bloc. It is unfortunately reinforced by the Western approach that I have just mentioned.

Iconology as a specific subject essentially consists of what is also called, according to Leonid Ouspensky, the "Theology of the Icon." This concerns the theological foundations of the icon, which explain both its content and its form, and justifies the ways it is venerated. This involves studying the history of dogma, in particular: (1) the texts of the Fathers who took part in the controversies of the two eras of iconoclasm—St John Damascene, Patriarch Germanus of Constantinople, Patriarch Nicephorus of Constantinople, and St Theodore Studite; (2) the texts (Acts and Definition) of the Council of Nicaea II which provide solutions to the problems posed and the official conclusions of the Orthodox Church relative to these controversies and the theological developments arising from them; (3) the texts by Orthodox theologians and local Councils (Councils of Moscow of 1551, known as the "Hundred Chapters," those of 1553–1554 and of 1666–1667) which had to deal with particular theological questions posed by certain representations (such as the representation of the Father, the representation of Christ as the Angel of Great Council, the representation of divine Wisdom, and the representation of the Eye of God[94]).

Iconology must also point to the essential link that exists between the icon on the one hand, and revelation and dogma on the other. It must therefore teach the criteria of a dogmatically correct representation. That is, it is respectful of what we know about the Triune God, of Christ (and of the main events of His earthly life concerning the economy of our salvation), of the Mother of God and of the saints, the Tradition of the Church founded on Sacred Scripture, the Councils, the writings of the Fathers, the *Lives* of saints, and in general the living teaching of the Church passed down faithfully from generation to generation. It is to this end that iconology compares dogmatically correct representations with dogmatically incorrect representations, taking as a first example the iconography of the Trinity, where the differences between the representations of Western religious art and the representations of the Orthodox iconography (in the strict sense, i.e., "expressing the right faith") are particularly blatant.

Iconology must also apply itself to studying the symbolism of the icon, which is particularly important. The icon is on the one hand realistic (in that it is respectful of the reality it depicts) but is not necessarily naturalistic and always has an important symbolic dimension. This is expressed at different levels, concerns different aspects, and takes various forms. For example, in the icon of the Trinity of Saint Andrei Rublev, which has become the essential model for all icons of the Trinity, a certain number of truths concerning the Trinity are expressed: the existence of three distinct Hypostases, their common nature, their loving relationship. But at the same time there is a strong symbolic dimension consisting in the fact that the Father and the Holy Spirit cannot be represented, the three divine Persons are represented by angels (these angels are the three angels who, according to the story of Genesis, visited Abraham and his wife Sarah and who were considered by tradition to be *typoi* [prefigurations] of the Trinitarian Persons themselves).[95] We can give another important example: the face and the body of Christ are divine-human because in Him the human nature and the divine nature are united without confusion and without separation. If it is possible to represent the humanity of Christ, it is not possible to represent his divinity other than in symbolic mode, in particular by the rays of the divine energies which emanate from him, which take a form analogous to that of light rays. With the representation of Christ serving as a model for the representation of the Mother of God and the saints, their bodies and their deified faces are represented in the same symbolic way. Other symbolic forms intervene to represent the minerals, the plants, the animals which, in the icon, surround Christ, the Mother of God, and the saints, and which participate in the divine energies which emanate from these and cause them to access a state which, while preserving their nature, transcends it.

There are in icons (especially in icons of church festivals) many dogmatic and symbolic elements which require explanations, which it is the task of iconology to provide, and which escape the understanding of simple art history. Good examples of Orthodox iconology can be found in works such as the *Carnets d'un iconographe* of monk-iconographer Gregory Krug, and especially in the *Theology of the Icon* by Leonid Ouspensky, which embraces all the aspects of the icon that I have previously mentioned, and highlights what distinguishes an Orthodox icon from a non-Orthodox religious representation. I myself, in a series of studies published under the title *L'iconographe et l'artiste,* have shown what distinguishes an Orthodox iconographer from an artist producing religiously themed representations.

Much work remains to be done with regard to these distinctions. If it is true that we have observed for several decades, throughout the Orthodox world—under the influence above all of Leonid Ouspensky in the Slavic sphere and of Photis Kontoglou in the Hellenic sphere—a broad return to the purest sources of Byzantine iconography, there are since in the late seventeenth century, in churches, vestiges of an iconography blemished through the influences of Western religious art, in certain cases even identifying purely and simply with it. Sometimes recent churches are painted in this style, as shown by the disastrous case of the Cathedral of Christ the Saviour in Moscow, for which historical restoration was preferred to Orthodoxy, thus giving, at the top of the hierarchy and with its authority (because it is the patriarchal cathedral), the worst example there is. Poorly crafted icons also often benefit from the piety of the faithful toward icons in general, and from the prestige that some of them sometimes hold from illustrious and venerable owners (such as the icon of the Mother of God of Tenderness before which St Seraphim of Sarov prayed) or miracles they produced: this seems to endorse their very style. In these ways we then forget what is essential: (1) that the prayer made before an icon is addressed to its prototype, according to the very terms of the Council of Nicaea II, and that the prayer of St Seraphim of Sarov gained its quality not from the icon before which he prayed, but from his own piety; (2) that the miracle-working icons do not possess by themselves a thaumaturgical power (it would be adhering to magical thinking to believe it) but serve as intermediaries to transmit an energy (a grace) which is granted by the person whom they represent (Christ, the Mother of God, a saint ...). It happens that miracles are produced through icons, the faces of which have been totally erased by fire, flooding, or other events, but which does not justify the existence of faceless images ... It must be remembered that ordinary material elements, such as water or oil, even if not consecrated, can also, when God so wishes, be vehicles of His grace. It should be remembered that the Orthodox icon always represents the face of Christ, of the Mother of God, and of the saints transformed by the divine energies (divine energies which Christ owes to his divine nature, and which the Mother of God and the saints received as a gift of grace), transfigured, no longer simply human, but deified, and in this divine-human sense, while Western art represents him as only human, and magnified only by a certain carnal beauty most often borrowed from human models who were not always holy (it is known, for example, that Raphael took his mistresses as models to paint his Madonnas, and other painters, like Leonardo da Vinci, took their homosexual friends as models to represent St John Baptist or other saints). Without going this far, the Orthodox iconographers of past centuries which were under the influence of Western art produced realistic or naturalistic representations, which while at times aesthetically beautiful, remained merely human.[96]

The fact is that icons have, by their mode of representation, an important pedagogical role, not only to make known to the faithful such and such a saint, or such and such a scene from the life of Christ, but to form the faithful spiritually by their very structure. Whoever prays in front of an icon painted in an Orthodox way becomes imbued internally, by an unconscious mimicry, with spiritual traits (such as the saint's concentration, humility, compunction, gentleness, compassion, etc.) that it expresses symbolically. Conversely, an icon that is not Orthodox, although not constituting an obstacle to the prayer of the faithful—nor preventing them from addressing themselves to the "prototype" or receiving grace from God to the prayer they raise in response—does not allow them to receive spiritual formation, and gives them a false and amputated representation of the divine dimension of the person represented.

It is therefore important not to place on the same level the icons whose style is canonical and the icons whose style is not canonical, and it is necessary to learn to distinguish them well. This is one of the tasks of iconology. This is a partly theoretical task, but also and above all a practical one. It is more intuitively than rationally that such a discernment takes place, through eyes trained by the habit of seeing canonical icons. Leonid Ouspensky, one of the greatest restorers of canonical iconography in the twentieth century, says that he and the future monk Gregory Krug (another hugely important iconographer of the previous century), having abandoned secular painting and wishing to train themselves in the best Orthodox iconography, assiduously frequented art galleries and museums to immerse themselves in the style of the most traditional ancient icons and draw inspiration from them in their own production. Today, there are countless works that reproduce icons from all eras that can serve as a support for such training under the direction of guides who are themselves properly trained and endowed with discernment.

Chapter X

The Study of the Canons

I have chosen to title this chapter "The Study of the Canons" to designate what is often, in Orthodox academies and theological faculties, referred to as "Canon Law." This latter designation strikes me as problematic: it is borrowed directly from Western Catholic theological faculties and institutes and is strongly marked by a legal conception of the canons of the Church, in line with the legal mentality which characterizes the Latin Church, and for which it is often criticized.

The corpus of canons in the Church is certainly analogous to the legislation which governs societies, with the particular canons analogous to the individual laws which constitute this legislation and which define obligatory or proscribed conduct. They too serve as a basis for judgments and sanctions relative to transgressions of or deviations from their prescriptions, but their application includes in the Orthodox Church a specific feature which is absent both from civil law and from the canon law of the Roman Catholic Church.

This specificity lies in the distinction made between *acribia* and *oeconomia* and concerns the second term of this distinction. *Acribia* designates a strict application of the canons, which is the same for everyone and in all circumstances. *Oeconomia* is a flexible, modulated application of the canons, according to the situations of the groups or persons involved. This variability, and especially the relaxed application of certain canons to certain people in certain circumstances, is quite surprising to the Western mentality and is often viewed as laxity.

There is of course, in the application of civil law, a consideration of the circumstances and the responsibility of persons, that is, their degree of awareness and the extent of involvement of their will. The judgments of the courts and the sanctions they prescribe are also modulated by reference to previous judgments which make up what is known as "case law." They are also adapted by acknowledging, in various forms and to varying degrees, "extenuating circumstances" in favor of those found guilty.

Oeconomia is not, however, the same as the application of case law, or the recognition of mitigating circumstances. It obeys a principle which is not of a legal, but of a spiritual order. It has its eye less on the past and the present than the future. It answers the question: what is the (spiritual) good of the Church and what is the (spiritual) good of the person or group of persons involved.

It is this principle that governs, for example, the methods of reintegration or integration into the Church of groups that have renounced heresy or schism. The variability in time and space of these methods (which may consist of baptism, or chrismation, or confession accompanied by a renunciation of past errors and a confession of the Orthodox faith) often seems shocking to non-Orthodox outside observers, or even to Orthodox people who have a rigid view of the application of the canons and are unfamiliar with the practice of *oeconomia*.

It is also based on this principle of *oeconomia* that, on the personal level, the Church grants divorces to certain of the faithful, although in principle she strictly affirms the indissolubility of marriage and excludes divorce. The Church can indeed recognize that, in cases where the couple is torn apart and various remedies have been applied in vain, only the breaking apart of the marriage (in fact acknowledging that the marriage no longer exists) will be spiritually beneficial, while maintaining it will be destructive. Many other such examples could be cited.

It is such concrete cases, testifying to the pastoral and merciful practice of the Church which must, in the case of canonical studies, be studied, just as the canons established by the Church at different times must be studied and assimilated. Account must obviously be taken of the fact that the practice of the *oeconomia* is in certain cases the responsibility of the synod of the local Church, in other cases of the bishop, and in still other cases of the spiritual father or the confessor. It is the latter person, for example, who modulates, depending on the person, the epitimias (penances) prescribed during confession for certain sins. It is also the individual advice given to the different faithful concerning the application of the fasting rules.

We see here that study of the canons needs to be closely related to other theological subjects: Pastoral Care, but also the History of the Church (e.g., with reference to the way the latter has reintegrated or integrated dissident groups), the History of the Councils during which a large number of canons were defined, or again Patristics, since several series of canons originated with the Fathers and are found in their writings.

Chapter XI

Pastoral Theology and Homiletics

Pastoral theology (to which homiletics is usually attached) is a "practical" branch of theology, addressed specifically, as its name indicates, to "pastors" responsible for instructing and building up their faithful. This they do in form of catechesis of children and adults, and in the homilies given in the framework of the liturgies, but also by confessing the faithful in the best possible way and directing them spiritually via confession or private conversations. This subject should in principle also help them accomplish a mission that is too often neglected these days: that of evangelizing the non-Christian society around them.

There is in pastoral theology, in all the objectives that we have just mentioned, a strong pedagogical dimension, but also a rhetorical one. This dimension of rhetoric explains why, from the first centuries, the Fathers attached great value to profane rhetoric and had in most cases themselves benefited from prior training in this field. This training concerned not only the stylistic beauty but also the clarity and good order of the discourse, as well as the quality of its argumentation.

Pedagogy needs to occupy an important place in catechesis at every level and adapted to each level. But it must also play a role in the directives that the priest gives to the assembly of the faithful in his sermons (while taking due account of the multiplicity of levels of knowledge and understanding found there) or to the faithful individually in confession. It is also important when it comes to addressing non-Christians.

Pedagogics has become in modern societies a branch of "educational sciences," having therefore, in the secular world, a scientific pretension. Teaching personnel in secular schools, colleges, and high schools receive specific training, theoretical and practical, from institutes that are capable of teaching the methods defined by these "educational sciences."

These methods and their acquisition are certainly valuable, but we also know that, in teaching, factors come into play which are related not only to the mastery of a methodology and "techniques," but also to the personality of the teacher. Specifically his ability to communicate, to grasp intuitively the receptive capacity—not only intellectual, but psychic and spiritual—of his listeners and to adapt to it, the trust and sympathy he inspires, his personal conviction and inner dynamism, in short to what are called, also in the secular world, his personal "charisms."

We know that, in the ecclesial domain, the human charisms of the priest are important, but that his spiritual charisms are even more so. These concern the strength of his faith and his degree of spiritual perfection and more specifically, in terms of the relationship with others, to his capacity for empathy, compassion, and love, but also to his humility without which spiritual gifts are not possible.

These natural and spiritual factors are independent of theoretical or practical pedagogical training, and mastery of them cannot be acquired via the education system. The latter should not be overlooked, as it provides a useful basis; but we must be aware that this basis remains limited and will have to be supplemented and transcended. We must also be aware that spiritual charisms, when possessed at a high level and translating the presence of grace, include in themselves the principles of the best pedagogics. Witness the Apostles who, being modest fishermen on Lake Tiberias or humble craftsmen or employees, spread the Christian faith throughout the world. A similar witness is provided by saints with very limited formal schooling (a recent example is Father Paisios the Athonite, who only finished primary school), but nevertheless attracted crowds to them. Or again by the *startsi* who, without pedagogical or psychological training, knew how to address everyone in an appropriate manner with answers adapted to their state in life and personal situations, and with such force that they could immediately act on the inner state of the person and change his life.

Faced with the success of American evangelist preachers, or preachers from other sects associated with Protestantism, some have sought to model themselves on their methods. During the "1st International Colloquium on Digital Media and Orthodox Pastoral Care" held in Athens in 2015, an American Orthodox priest, director of the Orthodox Christian Network, said he had trained for two years in homiletics in a training center for evangelical pastors, who according to him were much better trained than Orthodox priests since they managed to gather thousands of people to their meetings, and in their television programs more than a million viewers. Analysis of their methods, however, showed that they make extensive use of psychological devices that appeal to emotions and feelings, as well as the promise of immediate benefits (such as supposedly miraculous cures). They also testify to a form of Christianity that is very moralizing, undemanding, and simplified to the extreme. These methods are fundamentally incompatible with the requirements of Orthodoxy. The latter does not confuse spirituality with psychology, grace with emotion, or the instability and superficiality of a feeling with the stability and depth of a spiritual state, which excludes any form of psychological manipulation of the audience but calls on the free conscience of everyone and for agreed ascetic efforts, which are the only way to achieve a deifying transformation of the person.

Some local Orthodox Churches have also entrusted the pastoral training of priests to business companies specializing in the "management" of groups. These are private, for-profit institutes with no connection to the Church, which also train business executives from the world of economics. For example, recently in the metropolis of Iași in Romania, those responsible for the training of priests brought in an American company, the Arbinger Institute, whose slogan is "Mindset drives behavior. Behavior determines results. We change the mentality," and which presents itself as follows: "The Arbinger Institute is a global training and consulting firm that helps individuals, teams, and organizations achieve breakthrough results by shifting from the default self-focus we call an inward mindset to the others-inclusive focus of an outward mindset."[97] Several priests legitimately expressed concern that their ecclesial formation should be entrusted to an institution that is not only non-ecclesial, but linked to the sect of the Mormons and draws inspiration from the methods in use in this sect. One can be justly surprised at the conception of the Church held by those who, by appealing to such an institute, consider that it must be managed like a business, that its clergy must be trained like business executives, and that its faithful, consequently, must be "managed" like the personnel of a business corporation. One can also be justly concerned about the fact that the methods taught by these specialized institutes often include techniques of psychological manipulation, applied to groups or individuals, which fail to respect people as such by preventing them from thinking for themselves and forcing their free will.[98]

To expect a revival or an increase in dynamism from secular methods which have a certain success in the world (in truth a relative and temporary success) is illusory.

The high demands that Orthodox Christianity requires of its faithful are undoubtedly one reason for the poor effect of its pastoral attention, but the very way in which the clergy presents these demands to the faithful is questionable and even more so.

In fact, apart from catechesis, which is generally reserved for children, Orthodox pastoral work most commonly takes the form of homiletics, in the almost exclusive form of commentaries on the texts of Scripture linked to the liturgy of the day. These commentaries can often be repetitive and insipid, given by the priest in most cases out of obligation and routine. One draws practically nothing from them for one's own spiritual life after hearing them and returning home.

Homiletics ought to have a more practical aim, be more specific about what the faithful experience in their liturgical and sacramental lives, and what they can expect to experience in their personal ascetic lives. If so many faithful rarely attend church services, it is because they do not sufficiently perceive what these offer to them. If so many people move away from the Church or do not adhere to it, it is because that they do not perceive the positive purpose of the Christian life, do not see what it adds to their life in the world or how it can transform it in a beneficial way. It is precisely this that priests should show in their catechetic work and their homilies.

What has ruined Catholicism in the West since the 1960s was that the Catholic Church, through the "aggiornamento" of the Second Vatican Council, by wanting and believing itself to be closer to the people in their modern way of thinking and living, only secularized itself until its own contribution became indistinguishable from that of other social or cultural institutions. From then on, the faithful found nothing more in the Church than what society offered them and felt that they were wasting their time there. Under the pretext of getting closer to the people, many priests and members of religious orders (like the Dominicans) abandoned their theology studies to apply themselves to the "human sciences," in particular psychology and sociology. Their studies of psychology or sociology were of no benefit to the Church, and they themselves often returned to the lay state, which explains in part the considerable drop in the number of priests in the Roman Catholic Church during this period. The result was that during the decades that followed the Council, there were practically no more theologians, a fact noted, for example, in France by the director of the "Theologies" collection at Editions du Cerf, at the time the main French-speaking religious publisher.

The modernist current, which advocates "openness," that is, the adaptation of the Orthodox Church to modern thought and way of life, would, if it were to become dominant, only bring the Orthodox Church into the same decadence as the Catholic Church. Let us not speak about the classic Protestant communities which, long since secularized, have practically no audience anymore, the only ones which are numerous and are developing being the evangelical communities, which are fundamentalist and anti-modern.

It is certainly necessary, in pastoral care, to consider the concrete political, economic, and social environments in which the faithful live. In so doing, the aim is, however, not to enable them to conform to the modern way of life, but to help them succeed, in their particular circumstances, in continuing to lead a Christian way of life, which is accomplished often not in conformity and accommodation, but in a form of spiritual resistance. This has been a clear principle for all the Fathers and for the Christian tradition since the origin of Christianity. The Church is in this world, but is not of this world, and the tension which exists between the Church and the world cannot and should not be abolished. This is what justifies the effort inherent in the Christian life, which is rightly called "asceticism" in the most general sense of this word, and which inevitably involves a portion of discomfort and suffering, requiring a measure of renunciation, but also, in a more elementary way, a certain distancing from this world whose values, goals, and way of life are largely foreign to those of Christianity. But how this suffering is the source of a greater joy, how this renunciation and this self-emptying are the source of an incomparable spiritual enrichment, it is precisely what pastoral care must make clear to the faithful who, for the most part, do not know why they do what they do or should do what they are asked to do.

This involves an explanation that cannot be purely "technical," but necessarily appeals to the personal spiritual experience of the pastor. While this experience that can be acquired only in the concrete framework of his parish activity—that is to say his life—the spadework may be carried out in the context of pastoral training by occasionally bringing in as outside contributors experienced priests who have had a certain success in their pastoral ministry—for example by increasing the number of the faithful in their parishes, by stabilizing and regularizing the religious practice of the same, by keeping in the Church the young people who tend to distance themselves from it during adolescence—and are able to communicate how they developed their pastoral skills.

The practice of confession, which plays an essential role in the spiritual life of Christians, needs to be the subject of serious preparation in pastoral training. The teaching he dispenses to his parishioners and the very nature of his relations with them are dependent on this training.

First, confession must not be understood, as it often is, as a formal practice that merely gives an entry ticket to communion, but as a means for the faithful to become aware of their spiritual defects (which are deficient states, passions, and not just occasional sins). This occurs through verbalizing them in front of God in the presence of the person of the priest, to obtain forgiveness for them, but also to undertake to overcome them by means of the advice given by the confessor.

Secondly, confession is the moment when the priest can best give the members of his parish personalized spiritual teaching, which, for this reason, has a much greater impact on their spiritual lives than the sermons, the most common faults of which I have evoked earlier. Allow me to give here a personal testimony: I became Orthodox in a Russian parish whose priest, Archimandrite Sergius (Shevitch), of blessed memory, never gave sermons, but passed on all his spiritual teaching to his followers by confession which was much more effective. I do not say this to serve as a universal model, because on the one hand he did not give sermons by virtue of a feeling of humility which was his own, and on the other hand he was a charismatic confessor, who had the gift of reading hearts and delivering advice imbued with the divine grace which inspired him and which acted immediately on the soul of the faithful penitent. I cite this example only to support my point that confession plays an essential role in the teaching that the priest dispenses to his parishioners.

Third, confession plays an important role in the nature of the priest's relationship with his parishioners. If the priest is welcoming to those who come to him, and if, during confession, he shows them his love by listening to them kindly, praying for them, and giving them positive advice rather than reprimands, and if therefore, in other words, he shows himself to be both humble and compassionate, he establishes reciprocal positive relations with these faithful parishioners. This contributes to making his parish, by means of the bonds of love, a true Christian community and not just a formal gathering of individuals.

One sees yet again in the preceding considerations that it is not enough to acquire simple techniques through abstract courses during general training, but that the personal charisms of the priest, in other words his spiritual quality, are essential.

However, this does not make basic training unnecessary. Such training should first of all help future confessors to avoid bad attitudes linked to a poor conception of the pastoral function in general, and of confession in particular.

This poor conception is more prevalent in some local churches than in others. In Greece, not all priests confess, but only those who are instituted as confessors by the bishop. A confessor is called in Greek a *pneumatikos*,[99] a term which in fact designates a spiritual father. A priest can only become a confessor/spiritual father if he is recognized by the bishop as having the qualities to exercise such functions. He must be mature and psychologically balanced, lead an irreproachable life, be capable of harmonious human relations, have listening, understanding, and empathy, possess a certain discernment, and have sufficient personal spiritual experience to be able to give sound advice to others. In Russia, the fact that priests are confessors from the outset poses a certain number of problems as some of them have the requisite qualities, others do not. Among the latter, some, because of their youth, lack experience; others, imbued with the importance of their person and their function, treat the faithful with haughtiness, have cold and impersonal relations with them, and often show themselves to be authoritarian and brutal (according to numerous testimonies of Russian faithful that we have collected). The Greek "system" is obviously better, and it would be desirable for the Russian "system" to approximate to it, but this is made difficult by the fact that, in the Russian Church, it is traditional to go to confession before each communion, which makes confessions numerous and therefore brief. But on this point also the system ought to be not only relaxed but reformed so as to allow fewer but deeper confessions.

In any case, confessors ought to be seriously trained in the points previously mentioned. It is probably not private psychology teaching enterprises that should accomplish this task.

Part of this training needs to be carried out by teachers who are able, through their own experience but also through the testimonies they have collected from the faithful, to point to the negative spiritual effects of bad relations between confessors and those whom they confess.

Another part should be provided by outside parties chosen from among confessors whose spiritual quality is unanimously recognized, and who are able to share their know-how.

But another and not insignificant aspect of training should be the study of the words and lives of holy confessors where their way of living is revealed. Even if, as the expression of their personal holiness, these cannot be the object of direct imitation, they can at least provide inspiration.

The fact remains, however, that confession is, both for confessors and for the faithful, a difficult exercise. A great difficulty of confession is that there is no one absolute model that can be referred to. There are different ways for the faithful to confess and for priests different ways to confess, and a certain degree of uncertainty in defining, on both sides, the best one. For a long time, formularies were established to help both penitents and confessors. For the latter, penitentials were composed in the Middle Ages[100] (of which the best known in the East is the *Nomokanon in fifty chapters* of John the Faster) and, later, manuals, the most famous of which is, in the Greek world, the *Exomologitarion* of St Nicodemus the Hagiorite. The problem is that these treatises were composed mainly with the aim of helping confessors to fix epitimias (penances), and to harmonize their nature and their degree between the different confessors. Accordingly, they attempt to list all possible sins, giving first place to the most serious, for the reason that they involve the most severe penalties. Unfortunately, it happens that priests still have recourse to such treatises, using them to question the faithful about the sins they have committed and which they are presumed either not to have identified as sins, or to have difficulty in confessing. In this way the faithful find themselves questioned from the outset about extremely serious sins of which they sometimes do not even know the existence. We have received testimonies from faithful returning from Mount Athos and from Russia who have been not only shocked but traumatized following such confessions. Learning about confession within the framework of pastoral training should first of all insist on the tact that priests must demonstrate in the framework of confession and impress on them that their role is not to question but to listen. There is of course a problem linked to the fact that a number of the faithful who have committed sins or faults do not identify them as such.[101] It seems to us that, to face this problem, one should teach the faithful, within a catechetical framework, to recognize their sins and their faults. Lists of sins have been flourishing in Russia since the nineteenth century, one of the best known being that of Metropolitan Antony Khrapovitsky.[102] But they are not without their drawbacks: they give a legalistic vision of sin and confession, lend themselves to making it an enumeration of specific sins constituted above all by actions (ignoring passions, dispositions, tendencies, as well as what the penitent failed to do) and do not sufficiently serve to form the personal consciences of the faithful.[103]

A question that arises is whether future confessors should be trained in psychology, more specifically in psychopathology. This question calls for a double answer, positive and negative.

It is obvious that a certain number of parishioners are affected by various mental disorders. In the countries of the former Soviet bloc, the way of life specific to communist societies generated many such disorders (linked in particular to the breakdown of conjugal and family life, itself often linked to alcoholism, drug consumption, and violence), which have been passed on to the current generation. Among those emigrating to Western Europe or North America, there are added psychological problems linked to uprooting.

As I have shown in several of my books,[104] mental disorders can have various origins, spiritual, psychic, bodily, or demonic. At times one particular cause is clearly dominant, sometimes several causes combine. There are cases where a cure can be obtained by treating a spiritual cause. Sometimes the admission of a sin and its forgiveness within the framework of confession can have an immediate therapeutic effect; sometimes the prayer of a *starets*[105] can permit a miraculous cure; the advice, but also the love and the prayer of a spiritual father can, after a certain time, enable the healing of a sick person. In cases—it must be said quite rare—where demonic possession is involved, an exorcism can free a person from his/her troubles.

Many times mental disorders are linked to toxic family relationships over which the priest has no control if he does not confess and counsel all family members. It is therefore legitimate to seek a family therapy solution entrusted to a caregiver specialized in this type of problem. Very often, psychic disorders are associated with bodily disorders and require drug treatment that the priest does not have the competence to prescribe, and for which he must refer the sick person to a psychiatrist. For mental disorders that have neither a spiritual nor a bodily cause, the priest can refer a person to a psychotherapist.

But a number of very important clarifications must be made on all these points:

(1) It is useful for the confessor to know how to identify mental illnesses, and therefore the acquisition of at least elementary notions of psychopathology is useful or even necessary for his future ministry.
(2) Although the confessor can help penitents to improve their mental state by helping them to improve their spiritual state insofar as this depends on it, he must not confuse his function of confessor and spiritual father with that of a psychotherapist, and he must not engage *a fortiori* in the use of secular methods. Some confessors have been tempted to practice a kind of psychoanalysis during confessions. I have shown in one of my books that there is a profound difference between confession and psychoanalysis, and that there is a great risk—not only theoretical but practical—of confusing or even mixing the latter with the former, or of substituting the latter for the former *a fortiori*.[106]
(3) When the confessor directs a patient to a psychiatrist or a psychotherapist, he must first ensure that the latter is Christian and conforms in his practice to the principles of Christian anthropology. In the book cited above, I have shown at length how the anthropologies of Freud and Jung differ from Christian anthropology and are incompatible with it, and why, consequently, the forms of psychoanalysis which derive from them cannot be used without serious risks for Christian patients.[107] Many other psychotherapies are also based on a conception of man (of his nature, of the meaning of his existence, of his health, of what, in his inner and outer behavior, is normal or abnormal) which is foreign and sometimes even contrary to the Orthodox conception of

man, and which is very often linked (without this always being apparent) to sectarian movements.

It is important, in other words, that future confessors be informed—and therefore trained—on these points, and it is certainly not those outside the Church who are able to do this correctly.

In any case, it should not be forgotten that confession and spiritual direction are above all spiritual matters. Confession is not intended to relieve the penitent psychologically (although it may have this effect on a secondary basis) and spiritual direction is not intended to give material advice (as has often become the case) nor to orient mental life as such. Future priests should be trained to refuse to respond to requests from the faithful who often seek to lead them in this direction. Although very often they feel obliged to do so in order not to give the impression that on certain subjects they remain without response, or so as not to lose the authority that the faithful attribute to them—wrongly—in all areas.

The purpose of confession is to enable the penitent to become aware of his sins, to be absolved of them by God and interiorly purified, and—according to the second aspect of penance, looking no longer toward the past but toward the future—to undertake to cease committing them and henceforth to live in conformity with the will of God. It is to this last end that the priest's counsels are directed. Rather than focus on specific sins, that is to say evil acts or thoughts to which confession is too often limited, it is necessary to consider the source of these thoughts and acts, namely, the passions, which are habitual dispositions or states (in Greek *exeis*). The passions were considered by all the Fathers as illnesses, which should first be diagnosed and then cured. The therapeutic character of the sacrament of penance is moreover traditionally recognized by the Fathers, by ritual and liturgical texts and, one might say, by the whole Tradition of the Church.[108] It is therefore particularly important that the confessor himself be a spiritual doctor, having a good knowledge of the full range of spiritual illnesses, of their various forms, their causes, their effects, and their interrelationships, and then of the spiritual therapies that are suitable for them. This knowledge can only be acquired by a serious study of the ascetic tradition as we know it from the works of the holy ascetics, who, in the course of long and profound experience, have carefully analyzed the passions and found the means of becoming cured from them. The works of these holy ascetics—especially John Climacus, Macarius of Egypt, Isaac the Syrian, Dorotheus of Gaza, Barsanuphus and John of Gaza, Isaiah of Scete—have been collected in the *Evergetinos* or the *Philokalia*. I myself presented a vast synthesis here in my book *Therapy of Spiritual Illnesses* which has appeared in many languages[109] and is used as a manual in many seminaries and by many confessors, and which the French theologian Olivier Clément once called a "Philokalia of spiritual therapy." The fruit of eight years of research and embracing all the ascetic literature of the first to the twentieth century, this work unveils the rich heritage of the Orthodox tradition concerning the intimate knowledge of the soul in its deepest and most subtle spiritual and psychic "mechanisms." This heritage, unfortunately little known, is in no way inferior to the knowledge accumulated by modern psychological science and has the advantage over it of being based on a centuries-old experience which has amply demonstrated its positive effectiveness.

We see here that pastoral theology needs to be taught in close collaboration with ascetic theology (which is too rarely the case), and moreover that ascetic theology presented from a therapeutic angle (which is a perfectly traditional and patristic view) must be taught in part as a section of pastoral theology. Ascetic theology being closely linked to patristics, we find here the organic link that exists between the various disciplines of theology, and in particular the fundamental role that patristics must play in all of them.

The internet and social networks (Facebook, YouTube, Twitter, WhatsApp, Instagram, Snapchat, TikTok, etc.) have become the most widely used means of information and communication in today's world, to the point of becoming exclusive among young people. They are increasingly supplanting the traditional printed media (books, magazines, newspapers) and even radio and television broadcasting.

By their capacity to combine text, the spoken word and image, by their speed, and especially by their enormous diffusion without limitation of distance and border, digital media have had a considerable impact. They can touch both Christians who make use of them and non-Christians looking for answers, who come across them by chance or providentially.

It is therefore with good reason that the Orthodox Church has long been committed to the use of these new means of communication, creating a multitude of internet sites publishing information, positions, reactions from readers and discussions, but also books of theology or spirituality, liturgical texts, choral scores, videos transmitting religious services, homilies, conferences, debates, documentaries, cartoons, etc.

Under the aegis of the "Pemptousia" magazine and website, linked to the Athonite monastery of Vatopaidi, two "International Conferences on Digital Media and Pastoral Care" have already been organized, gathering nearly 200 participants from twenty-seven countries and from all local Orthodox Churches.[110] These conferences demonstrated the importance and impact of Orthodox engagement with the faithful via modern technological means. However, they have also highlighted the various problems that can occur by the dissemination of the Orthodox religious message by these means—by the discussions related to it, the relationships that are established through the digital form, and also by the proliferation of sectarian sites or blogs reacting to the message that are run by marginal personalities, and so forth.

It is important that future pastors as well as lay people involved in parishes or Church institutions be trained to use these media, but also to discern their qualities and their faults so as to make good use of them.

It is logical and necessary that, as part of the teaching of Pastoral Theology, a special sector henceforth be dedicated to the study of digital media in the various aspects that they imply.

Without in any way denying the value and usefulness of new media, of which I am partly a user and occasionally a contributor, I, like many specialists, express my worries about their faults and their negative effects in a book now published in many languages: *The New Media Epidemic. The Undermining of Society, Family and Our Soul.*[111]

One of these shortcomings is the poor quality of the attention that they arouse, with several scientific studies showing that, on a screen, reading is done diagonally, with readers retaining only a small percentage of the text. For site managers, the temptation is great to simplify content as much as possible to make it accessible to as many people as possible, bearing in mind the little time and attention given to a page. There is also a great temptation to adapt images and videos to dominant aesthetic tastes, thought, and language. In the field of the Orthodox web and its pastoral aims, there is therefore a great risk of presenting the Christian message in an inadequate form, impoverished, distorted, or even disfigured. The technical nature of digital media involves the additional risk of bringing to the fore, in the design and production of certain audiovisual productions, actors who lack sufficient and appropriate training in the content itself.

To quote a typical recent example—which can be said to constitute a "textbook case"—the Russian "Academy of Faith" (Академия веры) site offers cartoons with catechetical aims on different themes: "Who Is God?," "Why Is God Trinity?," "The Liturgy," "What Is Holy Tradition?," "Does Christianity Exist Beyond the Borders of Orthodoxy?" On the one hand, no doubt with the aim of capturing a contemporary young audience (and assuming tastes that perhaps—and even very likely—they do not have!) it uses simplistic and often-downright-ugly graphics, with icons themselves disfigured into sorts of caricatures. We are far here from Dostoyevsky's correct idea that "it is beauty that will save the world." On the other hand, with the aim of making complex truths of faith easily accessible, the site simplifies them to the point of distorting them and leading to downright heretical formulations, such as the use of the image of the cappuccino, composed of coffee, cream, and sugar, to represent the Trinity, an image that even a first-year theology student immediately sees is inadequate, since the three elements that make up the cappuccino are of different natures, while the three Persons of the Holy Trinity have a unique nature.[112] Heretical too, in a second cartoon, is the explanation of the Liturgy inspired by the ideas of the philosopher Nikolai Fyodorov, whom Fr. Georges Florovsky considered as "not being at all Christian and even contradicting Christian revelation and experience." In a third cartoon, the explanation of Tradition, shows it as entirely derived from Scripture (while Scripture is only one dimension of Tradition and receives its meaning from it), is borrowed from Protestantism. The question "Does Christianity exist beyond the borders of Orthodoxy" receives a relativist answer, drawn from the most superficial forms of modern ecumenism, also inspired by liberal Protestantism, which considers dogma as secondary, and places in the foreground a sentimental conception of love which is foreign to the spiritual conception that the Orthodox Tradition has of it.

What is amazing about this website is that it was created and exists with the blessing of the Patriarch of the Russian Orthodox Church, was founded and is headed by an archpriest who was until recently the director of the chair of theology of the Moscow Theological Academy, and receives input from several priests and teachers of theological disciplines. One can only wonder about the level of theological training of these leaders, but also worry about the so-called training that is given through such videos, because it is clearly akin to a distortion.

The realization of a catechetical project by modern audiovisual and digital means is useful, even necessary, but it requires a great sense of responsibility, and above all a solid theological basis, because it is extremely dangerous to simplify complex theological truths, and hazardous to try to explain elements of the faith which are of the order of mystery and do not lend themselves either to a rational approach or to a pictorial presentation. Catechism writers have known this for a long time.

The training of students in this area of digital catechesis presupposes a solid prior training in dogmatic theology, ecclesiology, iconography (and therefore also iconology), and also of all religious subjects likely to be treated. It also presupposes the acquisition of a sense of Tradition which is a sure guide in assessing potential new developments in the forms of exposition of the faith.

It is also important to learn to protect oneself from the influence of the dominant forms of expression, both linguistic and graphic, and to be aware that what interests people is not to find what they already find in the world and often disappoints them, but to encounter another world, more real and more beautiful. The Christian, it should be remembered, is through baptism a "new creature," who lives in a new society (the Church) and prepares to live in a world where all the imperfections of this world will be abolished (the Kingdom of Heaven). Traditional iconography gives him an image and taste of this. And it is also in this style that modern visual means must be oriented, which some directors manage to do, especially in cartoons for children or in films that cultivate beauty (which ancient philosophers considered the best support of the truth, and which convinced the holy Prince Vladimir in his search for the true religion, and which leads many people to join the Orthodox Church).

One of the tasks of catechetical theology is to develop this type of specifically Christian and Orthodox training, which elevates the soul both by its form and its content.

Notes

Introduction

1 As Father Georges Florovsky showed in his book *The Paths of Russian Theology* (Belmont, MA: Nordland Publishing Company, 1979), these influences were already perceptible in the sixteenth century and continued to exert themselves alternately thereafter.

2 Like those of sophiology inspired by Jakob Böhme and a whole "esoteric" current.

3 On the history and shape of these influences, see G. Florovsky, *Paths.*

4 See my book *"En suivant les Pères ..." La vie et l'œuvre du Père Georges Florovsky* (Geneva: Editions de Syrtes, 2019). [For a critical assessment of Florovsky's "western captivity" thesis, see *Georges Florovsky and the Russian Religious Renaissance* by Paul Gavrilyuk (2014) published by Oxford University Press—ED]

5 [The Bologna Process is meetings regarding higher education policy reforms between European countries to ensure comparability in the standards and qualifications.—ED]

6 We associate the two, because the former has been influenced by the latter, in particular from the nineteenth century onwards, and both have similar and partly common principles.

7 With regard to Catholicism, see the recent study by G. Cuchet, *Comment notre monde a cessé d'être chrétien* (Paris: Seuil, 2018).

8 Nor will we address the question (already addressed at the beginning of the twentieth century in Russia) of the audiences (clerics, lay people, future teachers, future researchers) that the various institutions address. Because if it is clear that the purpose of seminaries is to train future clerics, the answer is far from simple when it comes to higher education establishments.

9 H. Destivelle, "La réforme des académies ecclésiastiques et l'enseignement de la théologie orthodoxe en Russie au début du xxe siècle,"

Presentation of the PhD thesis defended in 2008 at the University of Paris IV—Sorbonne, p. 2.

10 Such sectarianism unfortunately leads some establishments to carry out purges of their teaching staff, these being directed today mainly by liberals against conservatives. It will perhaps surprise some, but let me recall this remark by Archbishop Lefèbvre, a traditionalist Catholic bishop ostracized after the Second Vatican Council and who therefore spoke from experience: "There is nothing more intolerant than a liberal."

11 As Fr. Georges Florovsky has shown, Tradition is not the simple preservation of the past, but the Catholic awareness (*according to the whole*) that the Orthodox Church has of its identity beyond time (see my book: *"En suivant les Pères ..." La vie et l'œuvre du Père Georges Florovsky* (Geneva: Editions des Syrtes, 2019), pp. 92–95.

Theology: Original Nature, Subsequent Evolutions, and Shapes

12 [That is, we do not know *what* God is (in Himself), but *that* he is and *what* he does (His *activities*). C.f. *Activity and Participation in Late Antique and Early Christian Thought* (2012) by Torstein Theodor Tollefsen. Also, c.f. *Letters* 234 and 235 of Basil the Great.—ED]

13 *De oratione*, 61, SC 589, p. 274.

14 Canons 19 and 64 of the Council *in Trullo*. According to Balsamon's commentary on Canon 64, the clergy themselves are in the position of taught and not teachers, in the same way as the laity.

15 See P. Georges Florovsky, *The Paths of Russian Theology* (Belmont, MA: Nordland Publishing Company, 2001).

16 See my study "Personne et nature. Une critique orthodoxe des théories personnalistes de Christos Yannaras et Jean Zizioulas," in *Personne et nature. La Trinité – Le Christ – L'homme* (Paris: Éditions du Cerf, 2011), pp. 207–396. [c.f. Louth's *Modern Orthodox Thinkers* (Westmont, Illinois: InterVarsity Press, 2015), especially chapters 12, 14, and 16.—ED]

17 Just as it is fundamentally foreign to the content of its theological reflection (see infra chapter 2, p.61).

18 [C.f. *The Cambridge History of Later Greek and Early Medieval Philosophy* (1967), ed. A.H. Armstrong. C.f. the first part of *The Fount of Knowledge* of St John of Damascus called "The Philosophical Chapters."—ED]

19 For example, at the Faculty of Catholic Theology in Strasbourg patrology is taught under the heading of "Ancient Christian Literature."

20 Many Orthodox Fathers profited from this, and Saint Basil the Great wrote a treatise entitled *Address to Young Men on How They Might Derive Benefit from Greek Literature.*

21 *Communitorium*, 2.

22 Multiple heresies that are found (sometimes inconsistently) in the new system.

23 See V. Lossky, "La controverse sur la Sophia." *Le Mémoire de l'Archiprêtre Serge Boulgakov et le sens du Décret du Patriarcat de Moscou*, Paris, 1936. [c.f. *Modern Orthodox Thinkers* (Westmont, Illinois: InterVarsity Press, 2015), chapters 2–4,—ED]

24 See my book *Personne et nature*, chap. IV, "Personne et nature. Une critique orthodoxe des théories personnalistes de Christos Yannaras et Jean Zizioualas" (Paris: Éditions du Cerf, 2011), pp. 206–396. [Regarding Yannaras and Zizioualas cf., *Modern Orthodox Thinkers* (Westmont, Illinois: InterVarsity Press, 2015), chapters 2–4,—ED]

25 Including Saint Maximus the Confessor who is considered to be a brilliant and particularly "creative" theologian. See my study: "La référence aux Pères dans la méthode théologique de Maxime le Confesseur," in *Communication to the twentieth International Congress of Byzantine Studies* (Paris: Sorbonne, 23 August 2001).

26 *De oratione*, 61, SC 589, p. 274.

27 Archimandrite Grigorios Papathomas, "La formation du clergé au sein de l'Église orthodoxe," Communication to the Symposium "La formation des cadres cultuels dans les Religions" organized by the Centre de recherches PRISME—Société, Droit et Religions en Europe, Strasbourg, 7 September 2007.

28 See *ibid.*

29 Cf. *ibid.*: "It should be pointed out that in the ancient Church, and even in the Church of the Romeo-Byzantine era, there was no university-type higher education, and the training of clerics was mainly carried out in the bishop's house, in the cathedral or in the monasteries, where they learned by example and by liturgical practice to assist the bishop in the celebration of the Holy Mysteries. This theological formation through liturgical practice represented the appropriate pedagogical method for teaching the Orthodox faith."

30 See Id., *ibid.*: " Before the seventeenth century, Orthodox theological teaching was based mainly if not exclusively on the writings of the Church Fathers of the first millennium, along with the Fathers until the fall of Constantinople in a unified way. "

31 See the reference study by G. Cuchet, *Comment notre monde a cessé d'être chrétien. Anatomie d'un effondrement* (Paris: Éditions du Seuil, 2018).

The Usefulness of Scientific Methods in Theology

32 For an article: author, title of the article, name of the journal, or title and author of the collection, number and year of the journal; for a book: author, title of the book, possibly publisher, city of publication, year of publication.

33 For example, the introduction to Cyprian of Carthage's *De Ecclesiae Catholicae Unitate* in the "Sources chrétiennes" collection contains an apology for the primacy of the pope, and the introduction to the *Homilies on the Our Father* of Gregory of Nyssa in the same collection an abusive interpretation of a passage in favor of the Roman Catholic doctrine of the Filioque.

34 See J.C. Larchet (ed.), *La vie et l'œuvre de Grégoire de Georges/Grégoire II de Chypre (1241–1290), patriarche de Constantinople* (Paris: Éditions du Cerf, 2012). [Available in the English language: Crisis in Byzantium: The Filioque Controversy in the Patriarchate of Gregory II of Cyprus (1283–1289) by Aristeides Papadakis (Crestwood, NY: St Vladimir's Seminary Press, 1997)]

35 See Nilus Cabasilas, *Sur le Saint-Esprit*. Introduction, critical text, translation and notes by Hieromonk Théophile Kislas, Éditions du Cerf, Paris, 2001.

36 See: Saint Gregory Palamas, *Traités démonstratifs sur la procession du Saint-Esprit*. Introduction by Jean-Claude Larchet (Paris: Editions du Cerf, 2017) [Saint Gregory Palamas, *Apodictic Treatises on the Procession of the Holy Spirit* (Arizona: Uncut Mountain Press, 2022)]

Dogmatic Theology

37 See my book *Théologie des énergies divines. Des origines à saint Jean Damascène* (Paris: Éditions du Cerf, 2010).

38 While for Roman Catholicism grace is created, for Orthodoxy it is an uncreated divine energy. It is only because it is uncreated that grace can ensure the true divinization of the Christian.

39 Giving rise to a "social theology," a "theology of revolution," a "theology of women," an "African theology," an "LGBT theology," etc ...

40 These currents are represented mainly by K. Barth, R. Bultmann, P. Tillich, W. Pannenburg, and D. Bonhoeffer on the Protestant side, and

by H. de Lubac, H. Urs von Balthasar, Y. Congar, K. Rahner, H. Küng, E. Schillebeeckx, and M.-D. Chenu on the Catholic side.

41 Represented primarily by J. Milbank, its founder and W.T. Cavanaugh, C. Pickstock, and G. Ward.

42 It is characteristic that neither Fr. Georges Florovsky, who had close personal relations with the great modern Protestant theologians, nor Vladimir Lossky, who had the same type of relations with great representatives of the "new Catholic theology," involved themselves in these issues of these modern theologians, but developed their work in the direction of an exposition of the most traditional Orthodox theology. See my study: *"En suivant les pères ..." La vie et l'œuvre du Père Georges Florovsky* (Genève: Éditions des Syrtes, 2019), and "Examen de quelques problèmes posés par des qualificatifs appliqués à Vladimir Lossky et à son œuvre" to the international theological colloquium devoted to the 60th anniversary of the death of Vladimir Lossky (1903–1958), Russian Spiritual and Orthodox Center, Paris, November 29, 2018, published in Russian: "О некоторых проблемах, связанных с характеристикой наследия Владимира Лосского," Вопросы Теологии, vol. 1, no 2, 2019, pp. 199–220.

Sacred Scripture and Its Exegesis

43 The presentation of the course in exegesis in the program of the Protestant Faculty of Strasbourg is characteristic in this respect, making the very content of the text appear to be quite secondary: "Among the many possible approaches to biblical texts, historical exegesis is unavoidable because it makes it possible to approach the conditions (material, political, social, cultural, etc.) in which the texts saw the light of day, and which forged the literary forms and content that we can observe and interpret today. This course, considered in a practical way, aims to lay the foundations of such an approach, using analytical tools that are essential in the context of a historical study: textual criticism, structural analysis, semantic analysis, tradition analysis, and editorial analysis. Together, the results of these different analyzes make it possible to construct a reflection on the function of texts in their contexts of composition and initial reception."

44 Historicism is a philosophical doctrine that asserts that the knowledge, currents of thought, or values of a society are determined by a contextual historical situation.

45 A good exposition of the patristic and Orthodox conception of the relationship between the Old and New Testaments can be found in the article by Fr. Georges Florovsky "The Fathers of the Church and the Old Testament." French translation in J.C. Larchet, *"En suivant les Pères …." La vie et l'œuvre du Père Georges Florovsky* (Genève: Éditions des Syrtes), pp. 312–319. See also, by the same author, "Révélation et interprétation," *ibid.*, pp. 363–383.

46 [The Septuagint is the translation of the Hebrew bible into Greek undertaken by and for the Jewish community in Egypt in the third and second centuries BC.__Trans.]

47 "Continuités et ruptures dans la théologie russe," section I.

48 The Fathers of the Church and the Old Testament (from the Collected Works of George Florovsky, Vol IV, Aspects of Church History, Nordland Pub. Co., Belmont, Massachusetts, 1975, pp. 31–38)

49 If, within Protestantism, the evangelical current has escaped this decadence and, on the contrary, experienced exponential growth, it is because it has not been associated with this project, adopting a fundamentalist approach toward the Scriptures. Of course, its success is not enough to legitimize such an approach, which is in no way that of Orthodoxy, which favors the symbolic meaning over the historical and literal meaning (see *below*) and is therefore distinct from both the fundamentalist approach and the modernist approach of Western denominations.

50 Cf. *De Principiis*, IV, 11

Patrology

51 Founded by Ferdinand de Saussure.

52 See my study: "La référence aux Pères dans la méthode théologique de Maxime le Confesseur," *Communication au XXe Congrès international des Études byzantines* (Paris: Sorbonne, 23 August 2001).

53 *Disputatio cum Pyrrho*, PG 91, 297AB.

54 *Opuscula theologica et polemica*, 19, PG 91, 225A.

55 *Letters*, 15, PG 91, 576A.

56 *Letters*, 13, PG 91, 532C.

57 *Letters*, 13, PG 91, 513C, 525C; 15, 545A; *Opuscula theologica et polemica*, 7, PG 91, 73C; 26, PG 91, 276AB.

58 *Ambigua ad Iohannem*, 42, PG 91, 1324D; *Th. et pol.*, 20, PG 91, 252C.

59 *Opuscula theologica et polemica*, 24, PG 91, 269B; 25, 272B.

60 *Letters*, 112, PG 91, 472CD; 15, PG 91, 565D; *Th. Pol.*, 20, PG 91, 249D.

61 *Opuscula theologica et polemica*, 16, PG 91, 185D

62 *Letters*, 112, PG 91, 484B.

63 *Opuscula theologica et polemica*, 20, PG 91, 245A.

64 *Letters*, 15, PG 91, 544D.

65 *Exact Exposition of the Orthodox Faith*, I, 1, SC 535, p. 138.

66 About which Fr. Georges Florovsky noted: "Evdokimov continues the tradition of Father Sergei Bulgakov; he does not follow the spirit of the Holy Fathers despite the fact that he quotes them" (Letter to S. Tyszkiewicz of 17 December 1960).

67 Piety is frowned upon not only in Western Protestant and Catholic theological schools, but by some Orthodox theologians influenced by their spirit. Thus, in a Russian blog, we saw a well-known theologian criticize his colleagues at Saint Tikhon's Theological University for being "pious people."

68 [The Bologna Process is meetings regarding higher education policy reforms between European countries to ensure comparability in the standards and qualifications.—ED]

69 In this order of ideas, it is paradoxical that in recent years, the manifestly heretical aspects of a part of the work recently discovered and attributed to Saint Isaac the Syrian have received greater attention than his Orthodox spiritual writings approved by Tradition.

70 This is the case for Dionysius the Areopagite, whose work is considered as massively testifying to a neoplatonic influence and whom one even identifies as a neoplatonic author, without understanding that he used neoplatonic conceptual frameworks as a Trojan horse to penetrate neoplatonic circles in order to lead them to Christianity from within by Christianizing their system (see in this regard the excellent study by A. Golitzin, *Et introibo ad altare Dei:* The Mystagogy of Dionysius Areopagita, *with special reference to its predecessors in the Eastern Christian Tradition*, Thessaloniki, 1994, and various related studies by the same author). The same applies to Saint Macarius of Egypt, whom a certain number of Catholic authors have endeavored to present as a Messalian under the title of "Pseudo-Macarius," identifying him with Symeon of Mesopotamia, an identification based on questionable assumptions. The position of these Catholic authors is in several cases openly linked to an anti-Palamite perspective and at the same time seeks to attach Gregory Palamas to the Messalian and the Bogomil currents. Certain Russian theologians belonging to the anti-Palamite current (like A. Dunaev) have unfortunately relayed the position of these Catholic

authors. For an update on this subject, see my article "Messalianism," in P. Sbalchiero (ed.), *Dictionnaire des miracles et de l'extraordinaire chrétiens* (Paris: Editions Fayard, 2002), pp. 524–527.

71 For example, the studies of L. Thunberg or P.M. Blowers on Maxim the Confessor.

72 In the context of our own work, we have appreciated the objectivity of the studies of Jules Gross, Irénée Hausherr, Antoine Guillaumont, André de Halleux, or our thesis director, Pierre Maraval.

73 In our study on *La divinisation de l'homme selon saint Maxime le Confesseur*, we opposed a series of tendentious interpretations of Saint Maximus' thought inspired by a mixture of modern personalism and neo-Thomism. Catholic specialists not belonging to these currents, such as A. de Halleux and M. Doucet, have also criticized these interpretations.

74 Like, for example, the prominence given to the systemizations of Saint Gregory Palamas in certain studies of earlier Fathers.

75 Like, for example, the importance given to by Dionysius the Areopagite's apophatism in the theological thought of Vladimir Lossky. See my study "Examen de quelques problèmes posés par des qualificatifs appliqués à Vladimir N. Lossky et à son œuvre." Communication to the Theological Colloquy dedicated to the 60th anniversary of the death of Vladimir Lossky (1903–1958), at the Centre spirituel et culturel orthodoxe russe, Paris, 29 November 2018; Russian translation: "О некоторых проблемах, связанных с характеристикой наследия Владимира Лосского," *Вопросы теологии*, vol. 1, no. 2, 2019, pp. 199–220.

76 To give a personal example, in my extensive study on *La théologie des énergies divines. Des origines à saint Jean Damascène* (Paris: Éditions du Cerf, 2010), I have avoided any understanding and interpretation based on the thought of Grégoire Palamas, not even mentioning his name, but concentrating on the personal work of each author studied during the period considered.

77 See the bibliography given by R. Arnou, "*Platonism of the Fathers,*" Dictionnaire de théologie catholique, vol. 12, 1934, col. 2258–2392, already impressive in its day. Subsequently, the emphasis shifted to Neoplatonism; this has given rise to a multitude of studies.

78 As in the works of E. von Ivanka collected in *Plato christianus*. La réception critique du platonisme chez les Pères de l'Église, Paris, P.U.F. 1990.

79 For example, with regard to the themes of the deification of man and the divine energies, almost absent from the Latin Fathers from Saint Augustine onwards.

80 For example, I noticed in a reference work on Saint Maximus the Confessor that the commentator compared an expression of Saint Maximus to that of a neoplatonic philosopher, seeing an influence of the latter on the former, whereas this expression is found in Saint Gregory the Theologian and it is clearly from him that Saint Maximus (who quotes him a lot and considers him "the master") borrowed it.

81 See my study: *"En suivant les Pères ...." La vie et l'œuvre du Père Georges Florovsky* (Geneva: Éditions des Syrtes, 2019), pp. 74–79.

82 In respect of Saint Maximus the Confessor, see my study: "La référence aux Pères dans la méthode théologique de Maxime le Confesseur," *Communication to the XXe Congrès international des Études byzantines* (Paris: Sorbonne, 23 August 2001), and the precise references given above in section 3.

83 As we have shown previously by quoting Saint Maximus the Confessor and Saint John Damascene.

Church History

84 This is bound to give rise to mis-directions when applied in different areas of theology. One can give as a recent example the ecclesiology and the eucharistic theology of Father Nicolas Afanassieff, which strongly influenced those of his disciple Father Alexander Schmemann, and which are directly inspired by the historical studies of the Protestant Rudolph Sohm, a disciple of A. Harnack. The idea that the Byzantine period had deformed primitive Christianity and the desire to return to the latter give rise to conceptions of the Liturgy and the sacraments, but also of the ecclesiastical hierarchy, that are far removed from the Orthodox Tradition (in its continuity and its temporal catholicity) and appeal to an image of primitive Christianity reconstituted by often dubious hypotheses. See my study "Aux sources des tentatives de réformes liturgiques de ces dernières décennies dans certaines paroisses orthodoxes: les œuvres du Père Alexandre Schmemann et du Père Nicolas Afanassieff," *Црквене Студије/Church Studies*, vol. 9, 2012, pp. 397–408. Serbian translation: "Покушаји литургијских реформи у последњих неколико деценија у православним епархијама: дела Оца Александра Шмемана и оца Николе Афанасијева," *Црквене Студије/Church Studies*, vol. 10, 2013, pp. 389–399.

Moral Theology and Bioethics

85 One can quote for example the excellent course on ascetic theology (unfortunately still only in mimeograph format) that Mgr Athanase

Jevtić at the Saint-Sergius Institute in Paris in the 70s of last century, or my book *Therapy for Spiritual Illnesses*, used in a number of seminaries and theological academies.

86 An English term for augmenting the human body using various modern technologies.

87 See in particular my two books: *Pour une éthique de la procréation. Éléments d'anthropologie patristique*, Éd. du Cerf, Paris, 1998 and *Une fin paisible, sans douleur, sans honte …*, Éd. du Cerf, Paris, 2010.

88 Thus Jean-François Delfraissy, president in France of the National Consultative Ethics Committee (CCNE), said, in an interview with the weekly *Valeurs actuelles*: "Sometimes science moves very fast and society lags behind, sometimes society moves faster. Between the innovations of science and those of society, there is no right and wrong. There is a balance to be found which must be part of the notion of progress. […] We have an evolving society, so there is therefore a series of values that can evolve. The concept of value is relative. There is no absolute value." To the journalist's question: "Isn't it your role to say what is good and what is bad?," he answered: "I don't know what right and wrong are, and you're lucky if you know it yourself! In any case, the CCNE is not there to indicate where good and bad lie."

89 As we have seen recently in several European states with the promulgation of laws authorizing MAR (medically assisted reproduction) for homosexual couples or single women.

90 See my book *Une fin paisible, sans douleur, sans honte …* (Paris: Éd. du Cerf, 2010).

Hagiology

91 This edition appropriates the name "Bollandist" but lacks the scientific quality of the hagiographic publications of the Bollandists found in the journal *Analecta Bollandiana* nor even *Acta Sanctorum*; it contains many errors both in the texts and in the dates of commemoration. Much more reliable is the Benedictine series J. Baudot and L. Chaussin, *Vies des Saints et Bienheureux selon l'ordre du calendrier avec l'historique des fêtes*, 13 volumes, Paris, 1935–1959. Father Macarius of Simonos Petra, for whose *Synaxarion* this series is one of the sources, notes that it is, however, not free from defects: "in the volumes published after the war it took an increasingly scientistic, and even ironic turn with regard to the saints, reflecting the general evolution of the Roman Catholic Church at that time."

92 Searching recently, before a trip to Ireland, for a book on the saints of this land, I could find only one book with the main title: *Saints of Ireland*, but subtitled: *Critical analysis of hagiographic sources (seventh to ninth centuries)*. This book not only did not contain the Vitae of the saints of Ireland but was devoid of information on their very lives.

93 Which the Bollandists themselves, concerned with historical truth, recognize. See on this subject the excellent study by M. Van Uytfanghe, "Hagiographie: "genre" chrétien ou antique tardif?," *Analecta Bollandiana*, vol. 111, 1993, pp. 135–188.

Iconology

94 Such work is not limited to the past. In my book *L'iconographe et l'artiste* (Paris: Éditions du Cerf, 2008), I denounce a number of false icons that have appeared in our time, the best known of which is the icon of the "Holy Family" which, from Catholic countries, has spread to Orthodox countries.

95 Only by the Incarnation was the Son fully revealed and thereby the Father fully revealed as such; and it is through the incarnate Son that the Holy Spirit has been fully revealed.

96 See my book L'iconographe et l'artiste, Cerf, Paris, 2008.

Pastoral Theology and Homiletics

97 https://arbinger.com/

98 It should be noted that in the metropolis of Iași, following the disarray of part of the clergy, the experiment was stopped and its initiator assigned to other functions.

99 [A *pneumatikos* is one who is filled with and governed by the Spirit of God.—Ed.]

100 See: C. Vogel, *Le pécheur et la pénitence au Moyen-Âge* (Paris, 1969).

101 For example, in the communist period in Eastern countries, abortion was trivialized, and a confessor told us that he had confessed a woman who had had about twenty abortions and was unaware that she had sinned in doing this.

102 "The confession of sins according to the ten commandments" in *Confession: A Series of Lectures in the Mystery of Repentance* (Jordanville, NY: Holy Trinity Monastery, 1975).

103 For more details, see my book *La vie sacramentelle* (Paris: Editions du Cerf, 2014), pp. 295–311.

104 See especially *Thérapeutique des maladies mentales* (Paris: Editions du Cerf, 2007), and *L'inconscient spirituel* (Paris: Editions du Cerf, 2011) (English translation: *The Spiritual Unconscious* (Montreal, Quebec: Alexander Press, 2020).

105 [A starets is an elder recognized by the faithful as someone to turn to for spiritual guidance and direction. Through the ascetic labors the Holy Spirit has bestowed on the starets spiritual gifts such as healing or prophecy.—Ed.]

106 *L'inconscient spirituel* (Paris: Éditions du Cerf, 2011), pp. 173–185.

107 *Ibid.*, pp. 31–104.

108 See my book *La vie sacramentelle* (Paris: Éditions du Cerf, 2014), pp. 269–285.

109 Original edition: *Thérapeutique des maladies spirituelles* (Editions du Cerf, Paris, 6th edition, 2013).

110 See the organization's website: http://dmopc.org/.

111 *Malades des nouveaux medias* (Paris: Éditions du Cerf, 2016). Romanian translation: *Captivi în internet* (Bucarest: Editura Sophia, 2018). English translation: *The New Media Epidemic. The Undermining of Society, Family and Our Soul* (Jordanville, NY: Holy Trinity Publications, 2019). Russian translation: *сторона новых медиа*. Издательство Сретенского монастыря, Moscow, 2023.

112 The same cartoon has a falsified reading of the episode of the coming of the three angels found in Genesis chapter 19, the two angels coming to Sodom being presented as having been sodomized and carrying signs on which is written "#me too"!

Index